KU-082-086

‖‖‖‖‖‖‖‖‖‖‖‖‖‖‖‖‖‖‖‖‖‖‖‖‖‖‖‖‖‖

GEMINI
22 MAY – 21 JUNE

All Rights Reserved including the right of reproduction in whole or in part in any form. This edition is published by arrangement with Harlequin Enterprises II B.V./S.à.r.l. The text of this publication or any part thereof may not be reproduced or transmitted in any form or by any means, electronic or mechanical, including photocopying, recording, storage in an information retrieval system, or otherwise, without the written permission of the publisher.

This book is sold subject to the condition that it shall not, by way of trade or otherwise, be lent, resold, hired out or otherwise circulated without the prior consent of the publisher in any form of binding or cover other than that in which it is published, and without a similar condition including this condition being imposed on the subsequent purchaser.

® and ™ are trademarks owned and used by the trademark owner and/or its licensee. Trademarks marked with ® are registered with the United Kingdom Patent Office and/or the Office for Harmonisation in the Internal Market and in other countries.

First published in Great Britain 2012
by Mills & Boon, an imprint of Harlequin (UK) Limited,
Eton House, 18-24 Paradise Road, Richmond, Surrey TW9 1SR

HOROSCOPES 2013 © Dadhichi Toth 2012

ISBN: 978 0 263 90254 9

Typeset by Midland Typesetters

Harlequin (UK) policy is to use papers that are natural, renewable and recyclable products and made from wood grown in sustainable forests. The logging and manufacturing processes conform to the legal environmental regulations of the country of origin.

Printed and bound in Spain
by Blackprint CPI, Barcelona

Dedicated to

The Light of Intuition

Sri V. Krishnaswamy—mentor and friend

With thanks to

Joram and Isaac

Special thanks to

Nyle Cruz for her creative input

and

Janelle Cook for editorial support

ABOUT DADHICHI

Dadhichi is one of Australia's foremost astrologers and is frequently seen on TV and in the media. He has the unique ability to draw from complex astrological theory to provide clear, easily understandable advice and insights for people who want to know what their future may hold.

In the 28 years that Dadhichi has been practising astrology, face reading and other esoteric studies, he has conducted over 10,000 consultations. His clients include celebrities, political and diplomatic figures, and media and corporate identities from all over the world.

Dadhichi's unique blend of astrology and face reading helps people fulfil their true potential. His extensive experience practising western astrology is complemented by his research into the theory and practice of eastern forms of astrology.

Dadhichi has been a guest on many Australian television shows and several of his political and worldwide forecasts have proved uncannily accurate. He appears regularly on Australian television networks and is a regular columnist for online and offline Australian publications.

His websites—

www.astrology.com.au and
www.face reader.com

attract hundreds of thousands of visitors each month and offer a wide variety of features, helpful information and services.

MESSAGE FROM
❧ DADHICHI ❧

Hello and welcome to your 2013 horoscope book!

The key to any successful relationship is communication. This is no secret and relates not only to personal one-on-one romantic relationships, but relationships in general. During 2013, the transit of Jupiter through the sign of Gemini highlights the fact that communication is the foundation of happiness and understanding in relationships, and that if you've been avoiding talking, sharing your feelings or opening up to the one you love, you can't expect your relationship to go very, far can you?

Effective communication is a form of self-education in which you are open to listening to another's point of view, adapting yourself and at some stage changing your habitual psychological patterns to accommodate the person you love. This can also be translated to business relationships, political interactions and any other relationship in which we empathise and feel the other person's needs.

Many of us are so busy trying to change the world that we forget that a better world starts with our own selves, which is why I am highlighting the fact that communication and self-improvement are the starting point for improving the world at large. By avoiding this, we shift responsibility to someone else and ultimately become the victims of our own lives.

The deeper level of relationships has to do with sexual intimacy. Saturn in the sign of Scorpio points to the fact that the coming 12 months will test us in this area of our lives and we need to be conscious that physical intimacy is really only an extension of our psychological and emotional connectedness to others. It doesn't matter which star sign you are born under, these planets will affect all of us in much the same way. Of course, depending on your Sun sign, the way in which you deal with this will change, but make no mistake about it; communication and intimacy are extremely important keywords for this coming period of time.

Fortunately, Jupiter expands our awareness so this means we are more likely to be open to the possibilities of being ready, willing and able to meet people halfway and truly identify with where they are at. Once this happens, you will start to feel the benefits of true communication. But clear communication is not just about the words that come out of our mouths. It has more to do with feeling the other person's point of view and doing our best to compassionately understand what they are trying to convey.

This year I have made it a point not to focus too much on bigger picture predictions but rather to simplify the message by saying that 'charity begins at home'. In reflecting the true traits of Jupiter, we must endeavour to do our best by helping our nearest and dearest, listening to their needs and largely doing what needs to be done on the home front before we look further afield.

Education isn't so much about degrees, diplomas and other intellectual accomplishments as it is about developing wisdom through a sensitive understanding of the experiences that life brings us. If Jupiter is to be of any use to us during 2013, we need to be receptive to the most personal aspects of our lives and express the lessons through loving, intimate relationships.

I look forward to being of service to you and hope that these forecasts for the coming 12 months will be of special value in helping you shape your destiny.

Your astrologer,

Dadhichi Toth
www.astrology.com.au
dadhichi@astrology.com.au

❧ CONTENTS ❧

CONTENTS
CONTINUED

❖ CONTENTS ❖
CONTINUED

GEMINI
PROFILE

AFTER ALL IS SAID AND DONE,
MORE IS SAID THAN DONE

Anonymous

GEMINI SNAPSHOT

Key Life Phrase		I Think
Zodiac Totem		The Twins
Zodiac Symbol		
Zodiac Facts		Third sign of the zodiac; mutable, barren, positive, masculine and airy
Zodiac Element		Air
Key Characteristics		Multi-talented, a thinker, talkative, social, scattered, has diverse interests, loves variety and excitement
Compatible Star Signs		Gemini, Cancer, Leo, Libra, Aquarius, Aries and Taurus

Mismatched Signs		Virgo, Sagittarius, Pisces, Scorpio and Capricorn
Ruling Planet		Mercury
Love Planets		Venus and Jupiter
Finance Planet		Moon
Speculation Planet		Venus
Career Planets		Neptune, Jupiter and Mars
Spiritual and Karmic Planets		Venus and Saturn
Friendship Planet		Mars
Destiny Planet		Venus
Famous Geminis		Colin Farrell, Marilyn Monroe, Johnny Depp, Clint Eastwood, Paula Abdul, Kylie Minogue, Morgan Freeman, Mike Myers, Paul McCartney, Russell Brand, Elizabeth Hurley, Bob Dylan, Drew Carey, Lenny Kravitz, Heidi Klum, Courteney Cox, Natalie Portman, Angelina Jolie and Nicole Kidman

Lucky Numbers and Significant Years	5, 6, 8, 14, 15, 17, 23, 24, 26, 32, 33, 35, 41, 42, 44, 50, 51, 53, 68, 77 and 86
Lucky Gems	Emerald, peridot, diamond, quartz crystal, aquamarine and jade
Lucky Fragrances	Basil, sandalwood, thyme, peppermint and lavender
Affirmation/ Mantra	I am calm
Lucky Days	Wednesday, Friday and Saturday

GEMINI OVERVIEW

66 WHEN ONE DOOR OF HAPPINESS CLOSES,
ANOTHER OPENS; BUT OFTEN WE LOOK SO
LONG AT THE CLOSED DOOR THAT WE
DO NOT SEE THE ONE WHICH HAS BEEN
OPENED FOR US. 99

HELEN KELLER

Gemini has the most amazing mind and people can be fascinated by the way you switch from one thing to the other without missing a beat. Your interests are diverse and you like to take a bit of this and a bit of that and match them up so that they come together as a wonderful idea.

The downside of this remarkable gathering of ideas is that you overtax your wonderful brain and need to step back for a moment. Geminis, being highly-strung as they are, run the risk of spreading themselves thin by taking on too much and not always completing what they begin.

Geminis are known as eternal students, always wanting to learn—and they don't mind what the subject is. They are good at assembling a multitude of facts and then turning them into their next 'great idea'. However, they don't always stay with this idea to the end, but it doesn't concern them too much. What would concern them is not having the 'great idea' in the first place!

THE GREAT COMMUNICATOR

Communication is your number one asset, Gemini. Your knowledge of the written and spoken word is immense. You are constantly learning, have an incredible breadth of knowledge, and are able to talk to almost anyone about your views and life experiences.

A Gemini can often be found with a pen in one hand and paper in the other. They could be writing their memoirs, researching a new project or just putting their thoughts on paper. There are many journalists, writers and advisers born under the sign of Gemini. Their words make a lasting impression on those who come into contact with them.

You are quick to come to a decision and prepared to run the risk of losing an opportunity that is presented to you. You can, however, with greater self-control, find the perfect balance between speculation and careful decision-making 'with greater self-control,' if you can rein in your impulsiveness. Discipline brings great power and it will give you the ability to use your wit and intelligence to achieve almost anything you want in life.

The human mind fascinates you on many levels. You are intrigued by such topics as psychology, philosophy and self-help because interaction with others is such a basic part of your nature. Gemini will often have a suitcase half-packed, ready to set off on another journey. You thirst for new experiences and it doesn't matter if it is a long or short journey; your itchy feet will set you on the path of another adventure. Again, you have to watch out that you don't exhaust your reserves of energy.

Chatty Gemini

Geminis are energetic and clever, which is why people are drawn to you and your wonderful company. Your adaptable nature makes you interesting to others and you can strike up a conversation on the local bus route or a transatlantic flight.

Mercury, your ruler, is called Kumar in Indian astrology, which means 'young person'. With your energy and love of life, you will always seem youthful. Your love of fun and seemingly endless 'get up and go' will give the impression that you are nowhere near old, even in your senior years.

When things are not going to plan for you, Gemini, you tend to worry and start running around in circles. This is counterproductive for a Gemini, so get back on track as soon as you can. Don't let others derail you from a project as it is important to 'own' what you started. You must always be the master and not the slave of your thought processes.

20 | GEMINI

GEMINI CUSPS

ARE YOU A CUSP BABY?

Being born on the crossover of two star signs means you have the qualities of both. Sometimes you don't know whether you're Arthur or Martha! Some of my clients can't quite figure out whether they are indeed their own star sign or the one before or after. This is to be expected because being born on the borderline means you take on aspects of both. The following will give you an overview of the subtle effects of these cusp dates and how they affect your personality.

Gemini–Taurus Cusp

If you are born during the first week or so of Gemini (that is, between the 22nd and 29th May), your Gemini adaptability is nicely offset by the rock-solid Taurus. Your character and personality are shaped by your ruling planet, Mercury, as well as Venus, the ruling planet for Taurus.

You have an insatiable curiosity, high energy levels and a creativity streak, but this is tempered somewhat by the security required by Taurus. As a result, your imagination gives you a drive to succeed that is not dissipated by your day-to-day activities. By being born under the combination of Gemini and Taurus, your chances of succeeding on a material level are greater than if you are not a cusp baby.

THE REWARDS OF PATIENCE

As a cusp baby, you are a very sensitive and patient individual, and it doesn't bother you greatly if success doesn't come to you immediately.
You are patient and hard-working enough to wait for that achievement to come to fruition.

You are kind-hearted and will not hesitate to hold out a helping hand to anyone who needs it. You are gentle and have a practical approach to assisting others. With your kind words and direct way of dealing with things, you get right to the heart of the problem.

You have a great work ethic and carry out the most menial of tasks with the same care and precision you would adopt for anything else. You are a perfectionist at heart, mainly due to your Taurean influence. You are modest about your achievements, but the world would be a better place if you could rise above your hesitancy and share your talents with others.

Gemini–Cancer Cusp

If you were born between the 14th and the 21st of June, you will tend to display many of the traits of the Crab, Cancer. You will have the head and logic of Gemini and the heart and soul of Cancer. This combination gives you a more emotional and sensitive side and may make it difficult for you to choose between your head and your heart.

Cancer traits may show up in more temperamental moments, which is surprising because Gemini are normally cool and aloof and don't show their feelings readily. This is especially so when it comes to matters of a romantic nature. It may make your sharply focused decision-making a little cloudier. This could be an irritation for you, but it is only a by-product of being a cusp baby.

You are strong-minded, Gemini, but emotional issues can fog up your brain. Yoga or meditation—where you can chill out, learn to regulate your breathing and let your mind and emotions settle—will help immensely. This will also balance you out so that you are not swinging like a pendulum from one extreme to the other. Find hobbies that can stimulate your mind but still keep you at ease and able to rest.

SENSITIVE CUSP BABY

Cancer's connection to the Moon tends to heighten your sensitivity, so don't get too upset when someone makes a thoughtless comment. You don't take kindly to criticism, even if it is constructive, and tend to see it as an attack on your nature and intention to do well by the world.

The emotional side of Cancer will give you an openness and warmth that others may take advantage of. You are generally perceptive when it comes to choosing friends and your intuition will rarely let you down.

GEMINI CELEBRITIES

FAMOUS MALE:
RUSSELL BRAND

Russell Brand was born in Grays, Essex, the only child of Barbara Elizabeth and photographer Ronald Henry Brand. His parents separated when he was 6 months old and he was raised by his mother. He describes his childhood as isolated and lonely. When Brand was seven years old, he was sexually abused by a tutor. When he was eight years old, his mother got uterine cancer and a year later breast cancer. He stayed with relatives while his mother underwent treatment.

At the age of 16, Brand left home because of differences with his mother's live-in partner. During this time he began using recreational drugs such as cannabis, amphetamines, LSD and ecstasy.

Brand is a former heroin and sex addict and a recovered alcoholic. He suffers from bipolar disorder and has been through a period of self-harm. He has shown an interest in the Hare Krishna movement and has been a vegetarian since the age of 14. Well known for his flamboyant bohemian dress sense, he is certainly not someone who fades into the wallpaper.

Throughout his life he has worked as a postman, stand-up comic, columnist, singer, author and radio/television presenter. He first achieved fame in 2003 as host of the *Big Brother* spin-off, *Big Brother's Big Mouth*. He got his first major film role in *St Trinian's* (2007), but his big break came when he appeared in *Forgetting Sarah Marshall* (2008), which then led to a starring role in *Get Him to the Greek* (2010). He has also been a voice actor in the animated films *Despicable Me* (2010) and *Hop* (2011).

Brand has been a controversial figure and was dismissed from MTV for dressing up as Osama bin Laden the day after the 11th September attacks in 2001. In 2008, the prank telephone calls he made to Andrew Sachs (best known as Manuel in *Faulty Towers*) while co-hosting *The Russell Brand Show* with Jonathan Ross led to his suspension and major policy changes within the BBC.

He married Katy Perry in October 2010 in India.

FAMOUS FEMALE:
ELIZABETH HURLEY

As a young girl, Elizabeth Hurley wanted to be a dancer and went to a ballet boarding school at 12. She later won a scholarship to the London Studio Centre, which taught courses in dance and theatre. During this time, Hurley adopted a punk-rock look with pink hair and a nose ring. To get work, however, she had to change her image to one that would gain her roles.

After finishing college, Hurley worked in the theatre and made her screen debut in 1987. More roles in television and film followed. She started dating actor Hugh Grant in 1988. Her film debut in a Hollywood movie was in the drama *Passenger 57* (1992). Shortly after this, she became headline news when Grant was picked up with a prostitute, Divine Brown. At the time, Hurley was representing the top cosmetics house Estée Lauder and the press pursued her relentlessly. She was soon replaced by supermodel Carolyn Murphy. Hurley and Grant went on to set up Simian Films in partnership with Castle Rock Entertainment.

As Head of Development, Hurley produced her first film, *Extreme Measures* (1996), which starred Hugh Grant.

In 2000, she and Grant separated amicably. Two years later, Hurley gave birth to Damian Charles Hurley in London. Steve Bing originally denied parenting the child until tests revealed he was the father. She married textile heir Arun Nayar in 2007 and divorced him in 2011. That same year, she started dating Shane Warne, the Australian cricketer.

GEMINI

AT LARGE

PLAY OUT THE GAME, ACT WELL
YOUR PART, AND IF THE GODS HAVE
BLUNDERED, WE WILL NOT

Ralph Waldo Emerson

GEMINI MAN

♂

GEMINI MAN: SNAPSHOT

Academic

Excitable

Motivated

Scattered

Humorous

In appearance you are generally tall and, if born in the earlier part of this star sign, you are also muscular and of an athletic build. Your face is usually long but in proportion with your body, with a high forehead and thin lips.

You are always on the go and tend to be busier than most of your colleagues and friends. You move fast, talk fast and can sell almost anything to anyone. Doing one thing at a time doesn't necessarily appeal to you and it is not unusual to see a Gemini male with several projects at various stages of completion.

In your relationships you can usually talk yourself out of difficult situations. Your need to talk can be quite overwhelming for a prospective romantic partner. You need to develop non-verbal skills so that you are not always communicating by words alone.

You are a loyal friend and respond with dynamic energy and speed to the needs of anyone you consider to be a friend. They can rest assured that you will always be there to help and this is indeed a wonderful character trait, Gemini. You are not afraid to offer advice, even when it isn't asked for, but you mean well.

As a Gemini male, you are never satisfied with your fame, reputation or money. You think that you deserve more, which is why you are not always sure you will be satisfied by what you get. You usually like sports and other physical and less intellectual activities. You may even try to hide your insecurity about your intellect behind a façade of false bravado and macho masculinity.

You like to stand out from the crowd and take great pride in expressing your individuality, whether it is in the way you dress or the way that you speak. Trying to ignore you is about as successful as moving a sand hill with a teaspoon.

You don't have any trouble attracting the opposite sex, but because you are always on the lookout for change, this may make any prospective partner a little nervous.

You love to be in love as it gives you a sense of security and there is the comfort of knowing that someone is going to be there.

You can be mysterious and don't like to reveal yourself all at once. Your partners may even feel that they are dating two guys at once because you don't want them to get to know you too quickly. It is more the thrill of the chase than the actual catching of the quarry that turns you on. Many Gemini males prefer to play the field and may not marry until after they have experienced a variety of romances, just to make sure that they have chosen 'the one' for them. When you do find someone, you are a cheerful partner, with a quick wit and great intelligence. You are gifted with words and have the ability to capti-vate a prospective partner's attention.

Adaptable Gemini

The Gemini male is very adaptable. This is due to the fact that Gemini is a mutable sign, changeable and malleable to the environment. With this trait you are able to overcome adversity and adjust yourself to the highs and lows that life throws at you.

You can also be quite restless and fidgety and seem quite inattentive. This is not intentional; it is just that you can't switch off and glide along in neutral. Sometimes, Gemini, you need to pause for a few moments, if that is at all possible, and think about where you are actually going and why. Focus is difficult as your mind can be quite scattered, but this is something you can master.

You can be the life of the party, Gemini, with a story to tell about someone or some place. Your conversations are never boring as you have an interest in politics, philosophy and other cultural and societal issues. However, you are a man with your own mind. You don't necessarily align yourself with the popular view and will go out on a limb with your own opinions. There is a danger, however, that you may come across as arrogant because you are well read on the subject.

You are always asking questions, Gemini, because you need to understand what is going on and why. It is from this well of information that you draw your well-founded opinions, and you can certainly be proud of your intellectual achievements.

GEMINI WOMAN

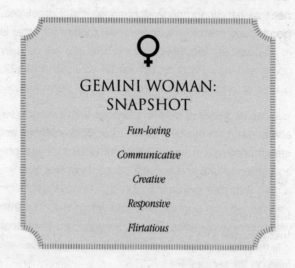

GEMINI WOMAN: SNAPSHOT

Fun-loving

Communicative

Creative

Responsive

Flirtatious

The typical build of a Gemini woman is tall, slender and very attractive. If you are born in the second half of Gemini, the slenderness may be more predominant. Those born in the earlier part may be slightly more curvaceous and fleshy. Gemini, you need to watch that you don't become obsessive about your looks or the appearance of others. You tend to take great pains to hide the parts of yourself that you don't want others to see.

Your mind is deep and thoughtfully provocative. When choosing a partner, you will need someone who understands your intellectual needs. You can be quite dismissive of anyone who is mentally lazy. They will also need to be caring, tender, romantic, reliable and have good manners.

You are ambitious and have the fast thought processes to make things happen. However, you need to be careful not to overreact to statements that others make. You can be hypersensitive and jump to conclusions, and sometimes you can be wrong. Yes, I know this is not an idea that appeals, but it's true.

You are socially very engaging and able to convey your thoughts in a way that is entertaining and witty. You have a great talent for stringing many thoughts together so that they make sense, no matter what their origin.

The term 'superwoman' springs to mind when talking about a Gemini female. Not for you the 101 tasks of a day, but more like 1001. You make friends easily as you are always happy to help out. With some brilliant time management, you can balance out your very busy life.

You were probably the inventor of 'multi-tasking' and were doing it way before the concept was recognised. Your hand shoots into the air at committee meetings and you can be relied on to at least start the jobs you have volunteered for, even if you don't always finish them.

You are quite capable of juggling a home, family and work, but should pay attention to when your fuel tank is running low, preferably before it hits empty. As your star sign regulates the nervous system, Gemini, you must be careful not to skip meals as this can undermine your health. Slowing down is certainly not something on your energy agenda, is it, Gemini?

Your coffee session with friends is just another way for you to expand your mind. You love to be with people who are interested in study, education, current affairs and self-improvement. It is likely that your social circle would include people with an interest in these subjects; otherwise you would have nothing in common with them. If an unsuspecting male is new to your social circle, he will be amazed at your razor-sharp wit and lightning-fast comebacks. Because you are well read, you are quick on the uptake on any topic and happy to chat for hours.

GEMINI CHILD

Your Gemini child is a curious creature, with a well-developed intellectual response to everything. From their earliest age, Geminis are inquisitive and keen to know just about anything; they will keep you on your toes with long lists of questions you won't have answers to.

Ruled by Mercury, your little Gemini is full of laughter, fun and practical jokes as well. It's a well-known astrological fact that you'll never be able to shut them up—they have to let you know what they're thinking (every little detail, mind you), as it helps them get rid of a lot of the nervous energy that is part of their character.

You will need to keep them busy with activities that engage their minds. This could increase your own brainpower because finding games, puzzles and other activities that are challenging enough will not always be easy.

To keep your Gemini child healthy, feed them regularly, with a good variety of fruits and vegetables and lean, low-fat protein. If you do this, your Gemini child will maintain optimum levels of vitality—physically and mentally. Because of their nervous energy, they have a tendency to burn calories even if they aren't active.

Your Gemini child will be bright and excel at school. They need to learn to tackle one task at a time, rather than skimming the surface of things simultaneously. They are full of beans and might burn themselves out, so take time to nourish them with good food, fresh air and outdoor activities. Of course, don't be swayed when they tell you they want to stay up to all hours of the night. Gemini children need adequate sleep to handle their busy mental overload. Problem-solving and subjects such as maths, science, communications, writing, singing and music are areas in which they shine.

As they get older and reach puberty, you need to be a step ahead of them. This is a critical time in their development when they may overstep the bounds of their mental and physical endurance. Be a friend as well as a good counsellor to them. If you can do so, your Gemini child will grow into a happy, sociable and productive member of society.

❧ GEMINI LOVER ❧

❝ THE MORE YOU LET YOURSELF GO, THE LESS
OTHERS LET YOU GO. ❞

FRIEDRICH NIETZSCHE

∽

When you are dating a Gemini, you will certainly need to provide stimulating conversation. If this is not you, save yourself the time and leave now. If you are the sort of person who wants a full-on relationship right after saying 'hello', then Gemini is not the one for you. Geminis can appear to be rather casual in relationships and want to develop a friendship before moving on to a more in-depth partnership.

If you want to attract a Gemini, keep in mind that their erogenous zones are their hands and arms, which are ruled by the star sign of Gemini. Light touching or even massage will make them more receptive to you and this can assist in winning their hearts. At the very least it will persuade them into a more passionate mood.

When Geminis have a small window of opportunity in their social calendar, and this doesn't happen very often, they can often be found having a coffee or a long lunch with friends or colleagues. They will, however, need to be great listeners, as Gemini tends to take centre stage.

At their best, Gemini can be joyful, good-natured, broadminded, experimental, radiant, friendly, enthusiastic, flexible and gentle. At their worst, they can be unreliable, fickle, insincere, self-focused, restless, critical and temperamental.

A Gemini lover needs to connect on an intellectual level before going any further. They want a friendship to develop and are not afraid to ask the hard questions in an effort to establish what makes you tick. Gemini in love may exhibit a possessive streak, but this is unusual. Boredom is a romance killer, so if you want a relationship with this star sign, you had better have some witty one-liners or at least read up on a subject that your Gemini is interested in.

Geminis have a great sense of humour and this sometimes gives the impression that their conversational style is a little superficial, but this is not at all so. It may even make you think they are not the least bit interested in you, but don't judge them too quickly. This is just their way of getting to know you. At times, Gemini gauges others on how much they are liked by someone else rather than really looking at their personality.

If you are a Gemini, you are intelligent, freedom-loving, versatile and at times erratic. You tend to be a romantic challenge to any potential mate, and something of a mystery as well. Your face is never blank and your expression is either lit from within or eroded by depression and moodiness. Your emotions are never at a standstill.

Gemini natives are children of the air and they need to feel free to wander, both mentally and physically. More often than not you may find yourself a bit lost and looking for the one individual who will fill that void in your heart.

A Gemini lover can be caring and thoughtful, but will take to the hills if they feel that the partnership has become too humdrum. However, if a Gemini individual finds a partnership that makes them feel whole and complete, then he or she will be the most dynamic and loyal of mates.

Passionate Lovers

Geminis marry for passionate love as well as for exciting and meaningful communication. They will sweep aside the advice of older and wiser people and go where their heart takes them. Those governed by Gemini are among the lucky few who know the deep expression of being truly 'in love'.

❧ GEMINI FRIEND ❧

Gemini, as a friend you are completely without any airs or graces. What you see is what you get. You have a great ability to make people feel comfortable in any social situation.

You have the ability to listen and are a wonderful communicator. Your spontaneity is endearing, to say the least, and although you can be unpredictable, it is this aspect of your personality that can keep others guessing—until they get to know you better.

You are outgoing, hold wonderful, stimulating conversations, and are open-minded in your opinions. You love to come up with a new idea, toss it around amongst those nearest and dearest, and watch it come to fruition. Boredom is never on your agenda, is it, Gemini?

You need to guard against the tendency to gossip. People will naturally tell you things and it is up to you to zip your lips when you know you should. If the story you have been told isn't spicy enough for you, resist the temptation to spice it up to make it more 'interesting'.

Geminis have busy social schedules and are sometimes overwhelmed by the amount of friends they have to keep in the loop. It is at these times that you need to look at the people in your circle and maybe weed out those who are not actually friends but more like acquaintances.

If you happen to be a possessive friend of Gemini, it is not a good idea to try and cage them. They will just spread their wings, like a butterfly, and flit off far away. You need to know that there is no way you can tie down a Gemini, so don't waste your time trying.

As a Gemini friend, you will be loyal and have friends for a long time, but you are also not afraid to try out new friendships as they come along. You like to travel and will meet people from many walks of life as your adventures unfold.

Gemini, as a friend you can be somewhat unpredictable, but underneath there is a good and solid person who will go to the ends of the earth for someone you regard as important to you. If a friend does the wrong thing by you, however, you will let them know in no uncertain terms.

GEMINI ENEMY

❝ IT IS DIFFICULT TO SAY WHO DO YOU
THE MOST HARM: ENEMIES WITH THE WORST
INTENTIONS OR FRIENDS WITH THE BEST. ❞

EDWARD G. BULWER-LYTTON

It is better to have a Gemini as a friend than as an enemy. Gemini, you are a wordsmith and will use your skills in this area as a weapon of mass destruction if the occasion arises. If you want to be on the receiving end of this vitriol, then cross a Gemini and you will get their venomous tongue in full force—and it's not nice.

For the most part, Gemini, you are polite and even-tempered, but if someone upsets you, they will find out about it very quickly. You are open about your feelings and opinions, but sometimes people will take you on because they think they know better than you on a particular subject. This is not a good idea. You will let them talk, although probably not for long, before you shoot them down with your superior knowledge and verbal dexterity. You also don't like people talking behind your back and this will bring out the worst in you. Back-stabbing is not a game you enjoy and it is one you do not indulge in. Although you may enjoy a bit of gossip here and there, you don't particularly like it when the tables are turned and you become the subject.

GEMINI
AT HOME

EXUBERANCE IS BEAUTY

William Blake

HOME FRONT

Gemini at home is the butterfly of the zodiac. You love to have space to move around in where you can change the furniture, alter the wall colouring or swap paintings from one room to another. Your home is the central meeting place for neighbours, friends and family.

Colours are likely to be a wonderful kaleidoscope of aquamarine, crystal blue, violet, yellow, orange and light green. Brightness is important, too, and your home will likely have large windows that can be thrown open for light and air. You generally like your furniture arranged so that conversations can ebb and flow. Groupings of sofas or a large table with many chairs suit your style of entertaining.

Geminis like their home environment to be neat and clean, especially the bathroom and bedroom. Your rooms will be a temple to taste and elegance with their richly patterned rugs and beautiful fabrics. You also like gadgets, Gemini, and your kitchen may look like a small-appliances showroom, but with your love of entertaining there is a fair chance you will use them quite a lot. Technology fascinates you and this is why you love the latest 'must haves'. Communication equipment will also be in abundance, with computers, mobile phones and remote controls for as many of your gadgets as possible.

City Slickers at Heart

Geminis are much happier in stylish city living than in a log cabin somewhere in the back of beyond. They like space, but it has to be space inside their home, not 100 hectares of front garden.

Textures within your home can vary from smooth as silk to rough as stone, but they will be tastefully included in a way that is unique to Gemini. Your main aim with decorating is to have a home that is totally 'you', no matter what the latest trends may be. Geminis hate untidiness and although they like plenty of space around them, it is not there to be filled up with clutter. They also like most things in pairs, or furniture with a geometric shape such as a square or oblong.

As Geminis have a great love of languages, it is likely that there will be a study or library tucked away that is used quite a lot. It could even be out of bounds to the rest of the household; a private space for the resident Gemini.

Working from Home

Geminis love their home and it would suit you to have a business that can be conducted within or attached to your residence. It would be a home which reflects the duality and variety of Gemini.

KARMA, LUCK AND
❋ MEDITATION ❋

In your past life, Gemini, you were highly progressive and intellectually very demanding. In this present life, you have adopted many of these traits to make you the forceful, dynamic and powerfully persuasive individual you are today. The lessons of your past life have taught you that intellectual arrogance and snobbery are tolerated by few. Unfortunately, some of you will not have grasped this facet of your spiritual development.

You have an intellectual and eclectic view of life, Gemini. You also have an incredible ability to communicate and most of your good fortune in life will come through this amazing ability. You are able to win over the hearts and minds of many people due to your communication talents.

The quality of air predominates in the Gemini temperament. Your mental and emotional equilibrium are related to your pattern of breathing, which needs regulating to lessen the level of anxiety in your life and bring you calmness and tranquility. Other methods of balancing yourself spiritually and emotionally include the use of gems and metals. The green emerald, silver or gold are useful metals and stones to tap the energies of Mercury and the Sun. The essential oils of sandalwood, Himalayan cedar wood, pine and ylang ylang will soothe your busy nature and bring emotional balance.

The Benefits of Meditation

You have a restless mind, Gemini. The day of Saturn is Saturday and it would be beneficial for you to meditate on that day. This will help accelerate your spiritual evolution and powerfully appease the negative karmas associated with your planets.

Your luckiest days are Wednesday, Friday and Saturday as the planets that are most friendly to you rule these days. Venus is your beneficial planet, which means that love and creativity, as well as some forms of speculation, will be lucky for you as well.

On a karmic and spiritual level, Aquarius has a strong influence on those born under Gemini. Developing your higher mind, controlling and directing your thought processes and not allowing the trivial issues of life to impact on you are all part of the natural, spiritual movement towards self-development and personal evolution.

Your key phrase is 'I think.' But remember, 'I think' does not mean to overthink. Focus on what you're doing and don't let your mind become the master. Rather, it should be the slave. Learning to balance thought with emotion is your challenge.

Lucky Days

Your luckiest days are Wednesday, Friday and Saturday.

Lucky Numbers

Remember that the forecasts given later in the book will help you optimise your chances of winning. Your lucky numbers are:

5, 14, 23, 32, 41, 50

6, 15, 24, 33, 42, 51

8, 17, 26, 35, 44, 53

Destiny Years

The most significant years of your life are likely to be: 5, 14, 23, 32, 41, 50, 68, 77 and 86.

HEALTH, WELLBEING
❧ AND DIET ❧

Gemini, nobody could accuse you of living life in the slow lane, could they? You are constantly on the move, either physically or intellectually, and it is a good thing that the winged messenger of speed, grace and versatility is your ruling planet Mercury.

Gemini is an air sign and dominates the airways, lungs, shoulders, arms and hands. You need to keep yourself warm and avoid illness, especially in the winter months, to avoid succumbing to asthma, bronchitis or other pulmonary problems.

Geminis are prone to taking on too many tasks at once and constantly rushing from one project to another to meet deadlines. Take care to avoid mishaps, accidents or other such unwanted stress by managing your time and eating smaller meals in an environment conducive to increasing your wellbeing. Sports such as tennis, swimming, walking or yoga, coupled with some meditation, will help to settle your mind and nerves.

Green vegetables are also an excellent source of dietary nutrition for you, mainly because this colour is predominantly ruled by Gemini. Although most foods agree with you, you have to watch that you don't overeat while you are busy talking. Lean, high protein foods are excellent for nourishing your body and sustaining you throughout the day. Oats and other raw grains, such as muesli, first thing in the morning are ideal staples for the Gemini character.

✾ FINANCE FINESSE ✾

Gemini, you have confidence that money will come from somewhere, somehow. This may be hard to explain to others, but it is true for you because this is what has happened in your life so far and probably always will.

As far as you are concerned, money is a necessary evil. You enjoy juggling many tasks and are ideally suited to being a salesperson. With your wonderful communication skills, you could, as the saying goes, sell ice to Eskimos. A freelance sales job is ideal for you as it gives the flexibility that you desire in your working day. Your charisma will probably lead to closing the deal, or the client might just sign on the dotted line to get rid of you. Either way, the money will go in the bank.

Changeable and unpredictable, you enjoy spending money and rarely worry where the next dollar is coming from, but somehow the dollars keep rolling in. You can't be bothered with balancing accounts since there are far more exciting things to do with your time. If your partner is willing to manage the purse strings, so much the better, because you are certainly not interested, are you, Gemini?

GEMINI
AT WORK

AS A REMEDY AGAINST ALL
ILLS – POVERTY, SICKNESS, AND
MELANCHOLY – ONLY ONE
THING IS ABSOLUTELY NECESSARY:
A LIKING FOR WORK.

Charles Baudelaire

GEMINI CAREER

IDEAL PROFESSIONS

Teacher

Mediator

Sales consultant

Inventor

Writer

Journalist

Tour guide

It would not be unusual for you to change jobs several times in a short space of time when you first start looking for a career. You are not afraid to try different things, but when offered a position that interests you, do some research before accepting the role. Geminis can also be employed in more than one position at a time. You can do a nine-to-five job to pay the bills, but then have a job at night or weekends that appeals to your particular nature. Your love of variety will have you moving from one job to another, probably for most of the early part of your life.

MIXING IT UP

Variety is the spice of life for you, Gemini. Your mind is constantly on the move and your career may reflect this as well. You are not looking for the gold watch at the end of 50 years of service as our grandfathers did.

With your mental agility and constant search for intellectual stimulation, you need to use your mind and rational powers to achieve the sense of satisfaction you desire in your work. Accounting, bookkeeping, IT, sales, public relations, advertising, secretarial, travel or editorial and journalistic professions are ideal for you.

Creative Gemini

As a creative creature, you need space to explore this side of your nature. Being stuck in a dusty cubicle, away from light and unable to communicate with your work colleagues, is not for you. This would be like a living death and would make you extremely unhappy.

Although you are not afraid to try new things, you do have a tendency to be a little overconfident in areas where you have little expertise. If this is the case, ask someone who has more experience or who is wiser than you so that this can add to your considerable knowledge.

If you are considering a managerial position, your employers won't have to worry about how you manage your time as you have the physical and mental energy to take on almost anything that is thrown at you. With your capabilities, Gemini, you'll have a successful and fulfilling professional adventure.

❧ GEMINI BOSS ❧

If you are working for a Gemini boss, don't worry too much about the procedures manual because today's procedure will be shredded paper tomorrow. A Gemini boss is a brilliant thinker, always restless and coming up with fresh ideas. They need employees who will just 'go with the flow'. As Gemini is a twin sign, it can be difficult to decipher exactly what your Gemini boss is going on about as you could be getting two different ideas about the same thing.

Gemini bosses can come across as thinking on more than one level at a time, and if you cannot immediately grasp the concept, you will get left behind. They have moved on to the next project while you are still trying to figure out the previous one.

If a disagreement or problem arises between you, the Gemini boss will appreciate you coming to them so that a speedy resolution can be reached. They like to use their reasoning powers to reach a mutually satisfying decision.

Gemini bosses will listen to their employees, but you must never try to outsmart them—their ego won't cope and you will lose in the long run. However, you can help them contain their energy as Geminis can spread themselves a little thinly at times.

A Gemini boss loves to talk and travel and enjoys being surrounded by subordinates and co-workers. They are a very social sign of the zodiac and lunch with clients will probably be in a restaurant. They have big network contacts due to their communication skills and like to keep in touch with everything that is happening in the business.

GEMINI EMPLOYEE

If you are casting your eye around to find the Gemini employee in the office or workplace, just look for the person who is juggling more than one thing at a time. That is usually a good indication that there is a Gemini on the payroll.

The Gemini employee has a spring in their step and a sparkle in their eye as they go about their daily duties. If they are not happy, they won't be working there. Geminis don't stay if their creativity and communication skills are not being utilised.

Gemini individuals always seem to have something to say, but there is generally a lot of wisdom or experience behind their opinions. With their love of words, they make excellent sales people and will come up with the latest company slogan. Give them the tools to express themselves and they will reward you tenfold.

Geminis can be a bit mean-spirited and gossipy if they get bored, but the idea is to keep them busy and out of trouble. They talk fast and move fast, so their work space needs to be clear enough for them to come and go without slowing the pace. They don't have a very good brake mechanism!

There is nothing a Gemini employee enjoys more than a brainstorming session. With their enthusiasm and creativity, it is right up their alley. They may make jokes and small talk along the way, but they will get things done.

Gemini employees love a fast-paced environment where things are happening all the time. They can, however, get a bit distracted by the details, which they see as boring, and the social activities that may be a part of the job. They need time to develop their skills and strategies, which gives them a springboard to come up with new ideas.

THE GREAT MULTI-TASKER

If you are a boss of a Gemini, get that wonderfully engaging employee on the frontline, give them more than one thing to do and watch them blossom. They are great front desk people and engage readily with whoever comes through the door.

PROFESSIONAL RELATIONSHIPS: BEST AND WORST

BEST PAIRING:
GEMINI AND ARIES

Here we have an air and fire element combination and this can make the sparks fly. The natures of Gemini and Aries are very compatible and if you are considering a business partnership, it would be hard to find a better combination.

Geminis are intellectually curious and love sharing ideas, which sits very well with Aries. When you blow hot, Gemini, and confront the fire sign Aries, you could have quite a firestorm happening. Your partnership is ideally suited for developing a good business and making it profitable in the long term. Aries falls in the eleventh zone to your Sun sign, Gemini, indicating profitability, friendship and the fulfilment of lifelong desires.

Not only could this be a successful business partnership, but it is highly likely that you will also be good friends. You feed off each other with your intellectual and physical drive and there is an ample amount of supportive communication and inspiration. These traits alone can be the cornerstone of a fledgling business that can grow into an empire—if you so desire.

Aries can be impatient or irritable at times, but you are more than capable of bringing them down to earth. Aries will appreciate the speed at which you think and act and, for the most part, you will be perfectly in sync.

You are a great communicator, Gemini, and Aries will appreciate this quality in you. You can provide a solid background and Aries will be the driving force for ideas to take flight and bring them to fruition. While you may take a little more time to think things through, you can give Aries direction, but make sure that your egos don't get out of hand. This is a danger for both of you, given your particular personalities.

Gemini, you are probably intellectually speedier than Aries, but not by much. Try not to outdo each other as the professional side of your partnership could suffer. You work so well together that there is no need for one-upmanship. You both have your own skill set, and once a common goal has been decided, you can go full steam ahead with the wonderful brains that you both possess.

WORST PAIRING:
GEMINI AND SCORPIO

Scorpio may fascinate you when you first meet, but beware. They may come across as the strong silent type, but for the most part they are secretive and uncommunicative, unless they have a good reason for showing their hand. Gemini, however, seems to have the uncanny ability of being able to get Scorpio to open up and communicate a little better. Scorpios are sensitive, extremely faithful and can be rather blunt, but they are controlling in every way.

A business partnership between the two of you would be prone to failure, Gemini, if you approach it with your usual casual attitude. Geminis can work with anyone on an equal footing, but the problem you will encounter with Scorpio is their driving ambition and instinctive need to dominate. This could make you feel uncomfortable in your work environment and stifle your creativity. As a commercial arrangement, there will be a battle of wills for power, and it is unlikely that Scorpio will back down; it is just not in their nature. You will get tired of always being the one to give in, even when you think you are right.

Your Scorpio partner will be brutally blunt. This may shock you as you are more diplomatic and use your verbal skills to find just the right word to get your meaning across without hurting anyone's feelings. Because Scorpio is not altogether trusting, they will want to know what is behind every idea you have before they will even agree to discuss it. This will eventually drive you nuts!

In a business partnership, there needs to be an exchange of idea, plans made and a myriad of other things to make the venture a success. You will have all your cards on the table, Gemini, and Scorpio will have theirs folded against their chest where nobody can see. This imbalance in trust will make you feel that they are being somewhat sneaky about information that is necessary for the functioning of the business.

Gemini, you would need to convince Scorpio that there must be open communication, trust and compromise for your business to survive. However, these three words may be completely foreign to your Scorpio partner.

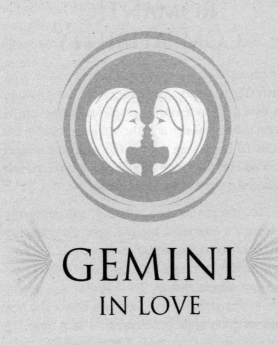

GEMINI
IN LOVE

THE EASIEST KIND OF RELATIONSHIP
FOR ME IS WITH 10,000 PEOPLE. THE
HARDEST IS WITH ONE.

Joan Baez

ROMANTIC
❈ COMPATIBILITY ❈

How compatible are you with your current partner, lover or friend? Did you know that astrology can reveal a whole new level of understanding between people simply by looking at their star sign and that of their partner? In this chapter I'd like to share with you some special insights which will help you better appreciate the strengths and challenges using Sun sign compatibility.

The Sun reflects your drive, willpower and personality. The essential qualities of two star signs blend like two pure colours producing an entirely new colour. Relationships, similarly, produce their own emotional colours when two people interact. The following is a general guide to your romantic prospects with others and how by knowing the astrological 'colour' of each other, the art of love can help you create a masterpiece.

When reading the following I ask you to remember that no two star signs are ever *totally* incompatible. With effort and compromise, even the most 'difficult' astrological matches can work. Don't close your mind to the full range of life's possibilities! Learning about each other and ourselves is the most important facet of astrology.

Each star sign combination is followed by the elements of those star signs and the result of their combining: for instance, Aries is a fire sign and Aquarius is an air sign and this combination produces a lot of 'hot air'. Air feeds fire and fire warms air. In fact, fire requires air. However, not all air and fire combinations work. I have included information about the different birth periods within each star sign and this will throw even more light on your prospects for a fulfilling love life with any star sign you choose.

Good luck in your search for love and may the stars shine upon you in 2013!

STAR SIGN COMPATIBILITY FOR LOVE AND FRIENDSHIP (PERCENTAGES)

	Aries	Taurus	Gemini	Cancer	Leo	Virgo	Libra	Scorpio	Sagittarius	Capricorn	Aquarius	Pisces
Aries	60	65	65	65	90	45	70	80	90	50	55	65
Taurus	60	70	70	80	70	90	75	85	50	95	80	85
Gemini	70	70	75	60	80	75	90	60	75	50	90	50
Cancer	65	80	60	75	70	75	60	95	55	45	70	90
Leo	90	70	80	70	85	75	65	75	95	45	70	75
Virgo	45	90	75	75	75	70	80	85	70	95	50	70
Libra	70	75	90	60	65	80	80	85	80	85	95	50
Scorpio	80	85	60	95	75	85	85	90	80	65	60	95
Sagittarius	90	50	75	55	95	70	80	85	85	55	60	75
Capricorn	50	95	50	45	45	95	85	65	55	85	70	85
Aquarius	55	80	90	70	70	50	95	60	60	70	80	55
Pisces	65	85	50	90	75	70	50	95	75	85	55	80

In the compatibility table above please note that some compatibilities have seemingly contradictory ratings. Why you ask? Well, remember that no two people experience the relationship in exactly the same way. For one person a relationship may be more advantageous, more supportive than for the other. Sometimes one gains more than the other partner and therefore the compatibility rating will be higher for them.

HOROSCOPE COMPATIBILITY
FOR GEMINI

Gemini with		Romance/Sexual
Aries		You may talk too much for Aries, but there is plenty of fire and excitement
Taurus		Constant stimulation is needed for this relationship
Gemini		Talking about what you want and how you feel will fill in many hours
Cancer		Sensual but difficulties with being rational
Leo		This could be the love affair you remember all of your life

Friendship	Professional
✔ Intellectually, this could be a first class friendship	✔ A power struggle
✔ Keep finding ways to keep this friendship fresh	✔ Taurus may come across as intellectually superior
✔ An enjoyable friendship if you can keep your egos in check	✔ Great creativity; always on your wavelength and mutual understanding
✘ Moody Cancer will drive you mad; you can't keep up with all the changes	✔ A good arrangement, but you will need time to develop a good commercial understanding
✔ Leo will appreciate your talent and friendship	✘ Leo can be somewhat stubborn and keeps cracking the whip

Gemini with		Romance/Sexual
Virgo		Virgo is too much of a prude for you
Libra		Libra really knows how to push your buttons
Scorpio		Great sexual chemistry and high energy levels
Sagittarius		Excellent match between the sheets; physically fulfilling
Capricorn		A sexual mismatch where Capricorn takes all
Aquarius		The sparks will fly with this match
Pisces		Pisces can make you happy on some levels

Friendship	Professional
✗ You won't like the constant criticism from Virgo	✔ Can be a great financial asset with their practical approach
✔ Intellectual, social and creative stimulation	✔ Long-term success can be yours
✗ Rollercoaster ride with this friendship	✗ You will need to stand your ground with Scorpio
✔ Social life will be No. 1 on the agenda	✔ Sagittarius can be lucky for you
✗ This will be like an obstacle course for you, Gemini	✔ You can do well financially, but creativity will suffer for it
✔ Be prepared to put in 110%	✔ Aquarius can teach you a lot about business
✗ Confusion reigns supreme in this match	✔ Pisces can come up with some great ideas for your business

GEMINI
❊ PARTNERSHIPS ❊

Gemini + Aries

A warm and exciting relationship as you love sharing ideas and this will stimulate you both. Gemini is intellectually curious and Aries will relate to this on many different levels. Geminis like to think things through, whereas Aries are more impulsive.

Gemini + Taurus

You have friendly planets in the zodiac so there is a natural attraction to each other. Humour, socialising and sharing your relationship with close friends bring you both tremendous joy. On an intimate level, your fast pace may become your undoing with a Taurus partner. You need to exercise some patience here, Gemini.

Gemini + Gemini

Romance with the same star sign can be a bit hit and miss. After all, there are two sets of twins at play here.

Although communication is a strong point, there's every likelihood that overstimulation will blow this relationship into an aimless affair. One of you needs to give the relationship some meaningful direction.

Gemini + Cancer

Gemini is the brain and Cancer the heart in this pairing. An excellent relationship if you can both compensate for what may be lacking in the other. Gemini, you may need to be more sensitive to what your partner is feeling, while Cancer needs to be more aware of what you are thinking.

Gemini + Leo

Air and fire—a good match astrologically. Like you, Leo is also intelligent, social and dramatic by nature. You will need to be on your best behaviour and look your finest to walk arm in arm at any social engagement with Leo. Great friendship is the basis of your connection.

Gemini + Virgo

Mercury rules both of you, but that doesn't necessarily guarantee a successful relationship. You may have similar ideas, but how you bring them to fruition is very different. Virgo's precision may drive you mad after a while. You are far more expansive and more of a 'bigger picture' person than they are.

Gemini + Libra

You are both air signs and this will give you mutual social stimulation, intellectual satisfaction and a creative friendship. This could be the start of something special. You will inspire each other to try for the bigger and better. Your love of art and music will give you a sense of harmony in the relationship.

Gemini + Scorpio

Scorpios come across as the strong silent type, but they are actually secretive and uncommunicative, except with Gemini. Geminis have the uncanny ability of getting Scorpio to trust them. Under their cold exterior is a seething cauldron of passion. There is no compromise in a romance with a Scorpio.

Gemini + Sagittarius

The fire of Sagittarius works well with the air of Gemini. Sagittarians are always looking for bigger and better things and you could be part of that journey. You too, Gemini, have a mental curiosity and you will intellectually stimulate each other. You can share great communication and have sexual compatibility as well.

Gemini + Capricorn

We have a bit of a speed difference here. Gemini is full throttle and Capricorn can sometimes seem to be in neutral gear. Capricorns are more concerned with issues of security than you, Gemini, and they may see you as a bit irresponsible. Not the best match of the zodiac.

Gemini + Aquarius

This relationship is compatible but also extremely challenging. You both have high energy levels as well as ideas and desires that need to be fulfilled, and this could place excessive demands on each of you. Aquarians can be stubborn and a little overwhelming at times, while you are more adaptable, but this relationship can work.

Gemini + Pisces

You like to think things through, but Pisces is off in some other place altogether. However, your spiritual connection with Pisces will allow you to feel sexually satisfied by them. This relationship can work positively because of your adaptability and the mystical connection between the two of you.

PLATONIC RELATIONSHIPS: ❧ BEST AND WORST ❧

BEST PAIRING: GEMINI AND AQUARIUS

At some time in your life, you will come across an Aquarian. They can be quite 'out there' compared to you, but somehow or other you make a friendship work.

Aquarians are unsurprisingly rebellious; it is just in their nature. They are quite aware of this but don't give it more than a nanosecond's thought. They are freedom-lovers, and as far as they are concerned, the world is theirs for the taking. They don't follow any rule book, other than the one in their own head.

You are rather in awe of this attitude to life and it reminds you that you, too, seek variety, excitement and intellectual development. Aquarians wring everything out of life that they can and you are amazed by the way they can do this and the freedom they acquire along the way.

You are both ruled by air and intellectually suited. Your Aquarian friend can be quite stubborn at times and thumb their nose at convention. For the most part, you'll be able to relate to them even if you do have a difference of opinion—and you will at some stage in your friendship. But you won't challenge them to the point of dispute and your differences of opinion will be in a playful tone.

With your mutual love of intellectual pursuits, you can often be found at a political gathering, cultural expo or a spiritual festival. You will never be stuck for something to do as you have so many interests and enjoy them together.

If at some time in this friendship you decide you want to take it a step further and develop a relationship or romance, you can do this with absolute certainty that it will all turn out all right. Your combination of Gemini and Aquarius can work just as well sexually as it does platonically.

WORST PAIRING:
GEMINI AND PISCES

Gemini and Pisces are not a good combination for friendship. You operate on totally different levels and would find it difficult to establish any common areas to get this relationship off the ground.

Although you, Gemini, can be moody and changeable, Pisces takes this far and beyond anything you have even thought of. They have a totally different emotional wiring and you won't have a clue what you are dealing with and will spend a lot of time and energy trying to work out where they are coming from.

Geminis like to speak their mind and are quite adept at communicating their thoughts. Pisces on the other hand, are not as forthcoming, and you will feel that they are holding something back. Gemini is intellectual and verbal, while Pisces is more intuitive. You both change your mind about as often as the weather, but are motivated in life by different things.

GEMINI TOO FLIGHTY FOR PISCES

Pisceans are more spiritual and may think you are a little superficial, Gemini. If you can show them that your thoughts and emotions run deep, you might be able to change their mind. You may come across as being a bit too flighty for their taste.

Gemini and Pisces can certainly have some adventures together, but there will always be ups and downs in this relationship. Rarely will you be on the same level, intellectually or emotionally. You are poles apart in so many ways.

SEXUAL RELATIONSHIPS: BEST AND WORST

BEST PAIRING:
GEMINI AND LIBRA

Here we have two air signs that are elementally suited to each other. Your personalities will naturally mingle, appreciate and love each other. You are stimulated socially, intellectually and creatively by your friendship with each other. These are the building blocks for something special.

You will have a natural flow of communication and you will feel free to express yourself in whatever way turns you on, so to speak. Libra is the fifth star sign from Gemini, which is regarded as creative, romantic and even sexually positive. As well as your minds being stimulated, your physical inclinations will be taken care of as well.

You both enjoy the company of friends and this is a natural bonding for you. Gemini and Libra are wonderful communicators and this is a strong point in establishing a partnership. There will be times, however, when you will have a difference of opinions and there will be no backing down for either of you. But the making up afterwards will be worth it.

Imagination and communication will be at the forefront of your dealings with each other. The humdrum of daily life is not for the two of you. You will inspire each other and continually reach for something bigger, better and brighter. You will both take pleasure in watching each other develop and grow together.

Air signs are culturally curious, if not artistically gifted. You both seek interests to engage the more refined aspects of your nature, such as art, music and even humanitarian work, which will give you a sense of connectedness to your fellow man. These pursuits will also bring harmony to the relationship.

NOT ALWAYS A BED OF ROSES

It would be unwise to think that this pairing is always joyous and peaceful. There are times when it will be anything but. Librans naturally try to find a balance, but may not always be successful, no matter how much they might want this. And you, Gemini, are not always in a state of equilibrium, are you?

Sexually, you stimulate each other tremendously, and you are also mutually affectionate. When you say you love each other that is exactly what you mean. For the most part, you are extremely well suited. There is certainly a natural bonding between you and there is no limit to what you can achieve together if you so desire.

WORST PAIRING:
GEMINI AND CAPRICORN

This is certainly not high up on the list of best matches, but there have to be some positives along the way. Let's try and find some, shall we? You have probably heard the expression 'less is more' and this is a case in point with Capricorn. There is a difference in both quantity and quality between these two star signs. Gemini is fast, versatile and adaptable in their way of doing things, whereas Capricorn is measured, slower and less wilful in their approach.

Capricorn can be far more conventional than you, Gemini, and they can sometimes make you feel stifled. They don't readily respond to your somewhat childlike attitude and it won't propel them into the more carefree lifestyle that you want. As far as getting them to be more progressive in their daily attitudes, you are basically wasting your time.

> *Gemini will often feel that their Capricorn partner is somewhat tight-fisted and worried about security far too much. It is difficult for a Capricorn to approach each day with an attitude of 'let's see how this 24 hours unfolds'. They are a bit more stitched up than you, Gemini, and don't have your carefree approach to life.*

If you are able to gain their trust by supporting them in their ventures and their need for security, you'll be surprised at how willing they are to meet you halfway once these needs have been met. However, this will be more to their benefit than yours, Gemini. This control may well spill over into your sexual pursuits where Capricorn could hold back in matters of physical intimacy. Capricorn partners need someone to help them unwind, but you, Gemini, may not want to spend the time doing this.

Gemini and Capricorn have different approaches to sexual intimacy. Ruled by the youthful Mercury, Gemini is rather light-hearted. This allows you to bring a lot of playfulness into the relationship, but it doesn't mean this will turn on the rather dour Capricorn. You'll need to give them time to warm to you and express the deeper passionate element of their nature, which is there but not always in evidence.

If you are determined to stay in this relationship, you may find that money—or the control and power it gives—will be a real sticking point further down the track. You will need to work on separating this from the sexual side of your relationship for it to have a small chance of working.

QUIZ: HAVE YOU FOUND YOUR PERFECT ❀ MATCH? ❀

Are you game enough to take the following quick quiz to see how good a lover you are? The truth sometimes hurts, but it is the only way to develop your relationship skills.

It is no surprise to anyone that we are all searching for our soul mate, the modern version of the knight on a white horse or maiden in distress. In the hurly burly of life, we might bypass that special one all because we are not looking hard enough.

You may be in a relationship that started off with fireworks but that is now burnt out. When will you know if that happens and what will you do about it?

If you are in currently in a relationship, are you truly happy or just marking time until someone else comes along who suits you better? Are you content with just one partner, or would you rather play the field?

When you are without a partner, are you happy on your own or do you feel as though half of you is missing and just waiting to be joined up with someone new?

Are you in a situation where you just don't seem able to find anyone, let alone the perfect partner? Are you looking in the right places?

As a Gemini, you're committed to intellectual understanding and communication. You need a partner who understands your need for connectedness at an ideas level. If you relate to your partner in this way, you have a better chance of success. You have certain unique requirements in order to be happy in your romantic life. So here's a checklist for you, Gemini, to see if he or she is the right one for you.

Scoring System:

Yes = 1 point

No = 0 points

- ❷ Does he/she have originality and versatility?
- ❷ Does he/she have a good sense of humour?
- ❷ Does he/she mentally captivate you, and keep you surprised and excited?
- ❷ Is he/she secure and open enough not to feel threatened by your quickly changing interests?
- ❷ Can he/she provide you with emotional stability?
- ❷ Is he/she passionate towards you?
- ❷ Does your partner give you enough attention?
- ❷ Is he/she proud to introduce you to the world, and show his or her love for you?
- ❷ Does he/she surprise you with thoughtful things like a hidden note or a holiday ticket for two on a beautiful island?
- ❷ Is he/she a good conversationalist?
- ❷ Is he/she open and communicative?
- ❷ Is he/she open to doing innovative things together?

❓ Does he/she make you feel excited every time you see them?

❓ Does he/she mentally and emotionally stimulate you?

❓ Does he/she go with the flow of your mind's explorations and journeys?

❓ Does he/she fall under the zodiac sign of Libra, Aries, Aquarius or Leo?

Have you been honest with your answers? Really? There is absolutely nothing to be gained here by tweaking the answers to suit the outcome. If you are aware that you are turning a blind eye to some things that are irritating or fall short of your expectations, then you will not get a real representation of your relationship.

Here are the possible points that you can score:

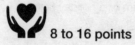

8 to 16 points

A good match. This shows you have obviously done something right. You have a partner who understands you, your life and your needs. But this doesn't mean you can just sit back and relax. There is always room to improve and make this excellent relationship even better.

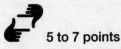

5 to 7 points

Half-hearted prospect. You are going to need to work hard at this relationship. It may require some good honest dialogue between the two of you, and honesty is the key word here. Go through the questions with each other and see what it is that's not allowing a better relationship to shine through. Is one of you too lazy or too domineering? After some time, do the quiz again and see if you rate your romance better. If not, it might be time to call it quits.

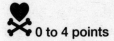

0 to 4 points

Washed up. There is insufficient mutual respect and understanding on this score. It's likely that neither of you is happy and that you have become too comfortable, like a worn out old pair of slippers. Is that what you want to be?

2013
YEARLY OVERVIEW

MAN DOES NOT SIMPLY EXIST,
BUT ALWAYS DECIDES WHAT HIS
EXISTENCE WILL BE, WHAT HE WILL
BECOME IN THE NEXT MOMENT.

Viktor Frankl

KEY EXPERIENCES

Vitally important astrological transits occur for Gemini in 2013 and many new experiences are forecast for you. The Sun, Pluto and Mercury activate the most transformative area of your horoscope, which relates to the most intimate areas of your life and, in particular, sexuality.

With Saturn in your zone of work and daily activities, these areas will be spotlighted as an important component of your development. Clearly defining who you are and what you want in terms of your career may not be easy, but it is essential in gaining success in whatever you want to do in the coming years.

Fortunately, Jupiter in your Sun sign is an important and positive element that can counteract many of the difficult and challenging planetary aspects that may occur during the coming 12 months. As long as you are prepared to redesign your life and adjust yourself to these challenges, you will experience an extraordinary uplift in your general affairs.

ROMANCE AND
❖ FRIENDSHIP ❖

Your relationships receive the sweet and beneficial influence of Venus as 2013 commences. This is one of the luckiest transits for you and highlights the fact that if you are prepared to work with your partner, spouse or lover, you can transform your relationship into something extraordinarily special. Matters of intimacy will also go under the microscope so that you can establish what you need to root out to make the relationship better.

January, February and March are very important months because Venus moves slowly upwards through your horoscope, touching important components of your relationships and professional arena. During these months you may experience strong connections with many different people. Of course, you need to figure out which of these are genuine and which should be discarded so that you don't waste your time on relationships that are not going to fulfil you.

Venus will be in the 11th zone of friendship and social activity towards the end of March and throughout April. You can expect some zany new connections at this time as Venus will make contact with Mars, the Sun and Uranus, highlighting the fact that there will be many opportunities to have fun, party, meet new people and enjoy an ever-expanding circle of social engagements. Be warned, however, that you may overdo it and end up tiring yourself out from physical and mental exertion. You must learn when enough is enough.

During the early part of May you may need to re-evaluate some of your relationships when Venus moves through the quiet and reflective zone of your horoscope. This doesn't mean you won't be engaged in relationships; it simply means that you need a little bit of time out to recharge your batteries.

In May and June you may feel as if things are returning to normal. Venus and Jupiter bring you a wealth of opportunities, good luck and a sense of exhilaration in all of your relationships. Make hay while the sun shines as these lucky opportunities are few and far between.

In August and September there are opportunities for you to commence a new love affair. Be careful of your choices as you may be impulsive and too idealistic for your own good. Problems may occur later in October and early November, which may be too difficult to undo. Think ahead before making any commitments.

By November and December you will feel a sense of completion and satisfaction with the way you handle your relationships. If you've had any sort of difficulty or long-standing issues, resolution can be achieved much more easily.

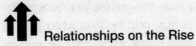

Relationships on the Rise

From the 17th of January you will need to carefully examine where your relationship is going. Issues of sexuality, finance and control may obstruct the free flow of communication and love between you and your partner. If you are unable to open up these lines of communication, you may set yourself up for more complicated difficulties down the track.

There's good news on the horizon after the 11th of February when Venus makes contact with your Sun sign. This is always an excellent time to showcase the romantic side of your personality and make good any difficulties that you have experienced in your love affairs. You will also feel generally attracted to the world around you. Make the most of it while this transit lasts.

You are extremely idealistic at the commencement of March when Venus and Neptune make you to see the world through rose-coloured glasses. Try not to see people for anything other than who they are and don't imagine things that aren't there.

A sensual and luxurious time can be expected when Venus and Mars do their sexy dance after the 7th of April. This is a pleasurable time and a great opportunity for you to explore and satisfy your sexual needs.

The wilful energy of Pluto may cause you some problems from the 6th of May until the 21st when you do something rather radical or out of character. Try to curb your impulses at this time or you may end up doing something that you regret.

Excellent romantic opportunities arise in June. Between the 7th and the 10th you will be excited about social activities and possibly even a new romance that may commence at this time.

With Mars aggravating your affairs around the 27th of June, be careful not to take out your frustrations on those you love the most. Issues of self-control will be paramount at this time and you must also be prepared to concede some small defeat if you are to maintain peace within your emotional and domestic environment.

You could feel cool in your affections to others between the 2nd and 8th of July. Saturn will perhaps make you project some of your insecurities on your friends and lovers. If your partner is not exhibiting the affection and demonstrativeness that you expect, break open the lines of communication and have a heart-to-heart conversation with them. Nothing clears the air like a good honest talk.

You can think big after the 22nd of July and take on big projects that include those you love. Sharing your successes and involving the ones you love in what you do is an important component of improving your relationships. Inclusiveness is the keyword throughout this period, but don't expect too much, especially around the 28th when Venus and Jupiter indicate that you may be demanding too much of those you love and thereby turning them off.

On the 2nd of September and then again on the 25th of October, Venus forms excellent aspects to your horoscope, highlighting the opportunity to step up your relationships a notch. Enjoy the warm fuzzy feelings with those nearest and dearest. You feel wild and unpredictable on the 15th of November and the influences of Venus and Uranus could set the trend for the coming 12 months. Be careful that you balance tradition with progressive attitudes.

WORK AND MONEY

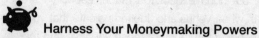

Harness Your Moneymaking Powers

Making money can be summed up in an equation:

$$m \text{ (\$ money)} = e \text{ (energy)} \times t \text{ (time)} \times l \text{ (love)}$$

If one of the elements above is not functioning properly in your life, making money may become all the more difficult. With the way the world economy is going, you need to do everything you can to improve your chances of being financially independent and secure.

It's always necessary to gain an understanding of all the universal laws of abundance and success when dealing with money. When fully present and creative, you inject the spirit of enthusiasm and love in what you do, be it work or play, and your aura or electromagnetic appeal becomes so much stronger. It is a force that attracts people, opportunities and, of course, more money. Your destiny and karma can be significantly influenced by the way you think and the attitude you foster. This will in turn impact upon your moneymaking powers.

Mars is the planet relating to profitability in June 2013 and we find this planet elevated in the area of good luck. This is not to say that you don't have to work hard for the money you learn throughout 2013, only that the effort you make will be rewarded in a much more timely manner than it otherwise would be.

Profits are up in the first week of January, but the 8th to the 15th might prove to be a little frustrating as your efforts are not as easily rewarded. Don't lose heart and try to be as constructive as you can in the way that you do your work. You have a spurt of energy once again after the 19th when Mars and the Sun energise you physically, which means that you can get a lot of work done and achieve some excellent results.

Your powerful physical drives continue and will be channelled into your work practices throughout February and March. Be careful at the commencement of this period, however, as Mars and Neptune indicate that you may be a little too idealistic for your own good. Keep your plans rooted in reality.

At the end of March and throughout April, when Mars makes contact with Uranus, the Sun and Venus, an unexpected windfall, profit or other wonderful opportunity may present itself to you out of the blue. It's at this time that you will also make new connections through friends and further capitalise and increase your profits in the future.

In May, June and July, take the time to negotiate what you want in the way of shared resources as you may be completely at odds with your business partners or romantic mate. Having a clear objective and a common dream is important at this time, otherwise you may be totally out of sync with them.

Take care not to be wasteful during August. You may suddenly want to spend a lot of money for the hell of it. Being a spendthrift is not the best way to build up your nest egg. Exercise caution.

Jupiter is very lucky for you throughout October when it enters an excellent relationship with your career zone. Explore each and every business and professional opportunity that is presented to you as it could be time for an elevation of status, a promotion or increased wealth.

Jupiter once again highlights the lucky vibrations for you in terms of your work and money on the 12th and 13th of December. As mentioned before, don't allow rash behaviour to neutralise the good results you have achieved in 2013.

 Tips for Financial Success

Looking a little more closely at your transits in the coming 12 months will give you the opportunity to see how you can make the most of your financial circum-stances. On the 4th and 19th of January, Mars and

Jupiter encourage you to take some calculated risks on your big dreams. If you never act upon your vision for a greater future, will you ever realise your professional and financial objectives? You may feel a little nervous about moving in a direction that is completely foreign to you, but once you start, you'll get the hang of it and enjoy a taste of success.

In helping someone achieve their success after the 7th of April, you will realise that your own success has been augmented through the process. Pooling resources with friends and co-workers could give rise to new opportunities in business.

Dare to be different after the 13th of June. You need to be progressive in the way you tackle your professional objectives. Venus will continue to spur you on to bigger and better things, but only if you are prepared to step outside the square. Take this concept a little further and look carefully at the opportunities that present themselves to you in speculative ventures, the stock market and other types of ventures. Without being a gambler, you can judiciously invest money and earn well without wearing yourself out. You can do so after the 23rd of September, when Venus, the Sun and Jupiter bring you some good karma.

Career Moves and Promotions

Between the 23rd of January and the 5th of February, there are good planetary energies for you to ascend the throne—if I can put it that way. Don't be shy in coming forward when an opportunity presents itself for you to take on a leadership role. You've worked hard, so why back away now when destiny brings you the opportunity?

The Sun, willpower and professional perfection bring you further opportunities between the 18th and the 27th of February. You'll be noticed for the good work that you do, so don't be too humble when someone asks you whether you are capable of handling the job.

If you are contemplating a radical move, such as relocating to another company, the month of May could be a time when you might even go so far as to leave the state or the country. There is a strong flavour of emigration, long-distance travel and professional moves that will not only improve your career but also give you a deep sense of self-satisfaction. This is a time for you to spread your wings and explore the world, as well as giving yourself a chance for promotion.

In June, the combined influence of the Sun and Neptune allow you to achieve what you previously thought was impossible. This could be a creative aspect of your personality that you've been too scared to act upon. There are similar aspects forming around the 31st of July, the 10th of August, the 27th of September and again on the 26th of October.

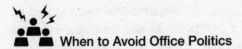 **When to Avoid Office Politics**

Life at work can sometimes become unbearable if your relationship with co-workers or employers is adverse. You need to sidestep or take control of the situation if someone is undermining you. Knowing when to do this will give you an advantage. It is likely that you may make some enemies this year, so you will need some strategies in your tool kit to deal with this.

Between the 8th of January and the 11th of February there could be open antagonism from people you work with. You need to use the power of Venus to persuasively win them over. It will be easy for you to retaliate and let your ego get the better of you, but this will not be in your best interests over the long term.

Worse than open enemies are secret enemies who conspire behind your back. Between the 15th and the 20th of April, read between the lines; someone may be trying to bring you down by quietly manoeuvring the situation.

On the 1st of May, the 2nd of July and the 9th of September you should make a point of carefully analysing the motives of those you work with or intend to do business with. There will be undercurrents of work politics and power games and understanding the rules of this game means that you will have the edge over your competitors. Don't assume that everything will be hunky dory if you turn away and leave people to their own devices. You need to take control under these circumstances.

Someone you consider a friend may turn on you or inadvertently undermine you around the 5th of November. Try connecting more deeply with your acquaintances to try to understand their motives so that you can sidestep political issues that will damage your relationships in the future.

HEALTH, BEAUTY AND
❧ LIFESTYLE ❧

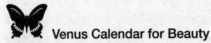 **Venus Calendar for Beauty**

The presence of Jupiter in your Sun sign this year is an excellent omen for good luck as well as feeling great and attracting wonderful opportunities both professionally and personally. Naturally, if you feel good about yourself, others are going to respond to you favourably.

Between the 20th and the 30th of January, feeling good also means travelling and mixing with people from different cultures who can offer you a different slant on life. By extending your circle of understanding with individuals like this, you will feel much better about yourself.

The Sun is the brightest object in the sky, and when it makes contact with your Sun sign around the 8th of February, you will feel an improvement in your physical vitality and people will see this. Capitalise on opportunities to make friends and show off your best personality traits.

Between the 4th of March and the 5th of April, your attractiveness will be showcased through your work and professional activities. Looking your best in these areas will ensure that others will treat you with respect and help you achieve what you have on your agenda. These are excellent cycles to forge ahead in your life.

After the 14th of April, Mercury creates a magnetic aura around you and others will palpably feel your beauty and attractiveness. You mustn't abuse this power as you'll be able to take advantage of others if you do so. Wield this power fairly and karma will bless you with wonderful friendships and new associations.

Between the 3rd and the 28th of June, beautify yourself by going to your local spa and having a facial, manicure or pedicure. Look carefully at your diet to make sure that the beauty you're trying to achieve is also happening from the inside, not just from a cosmetic point of view.

Being happy and creative is a sure way of firing up those beautifying endorphins within you. Between the 2nd and the 15th of September, get away from the hustle and bustle of day-to-day life and do something that really makes you feel good. Others will notice a glow around you.

When Venus passes through your seventh zone of the world at large, be sure to strike while the iron is hot. Any sort of contract, negotiation or deal, especially of a personal nature, is easily secured during this friendly transit of the planet of love and beauty. Finally, you have another shot at love and impressing others when the

Sun passes through the same zone of your horoscope. This cycle of love and beauty between the 22nd of November and the 24th of December is really hot and brings in its wake excellent love and sensuality—because you look so good!

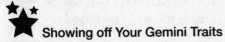

Showing off Your Gemini Traits

Each zodiac sign is unique and by understanding which character traits are your strong point you can use this to your best advantage over the coming months. For Gemini, your ability to communicate, share ideas and make your mark using the power of your brain is vitally important. How can you display these traits in 2013 and make a lasting impression?

From the first week of January, you're keen to probe the mysteries of life to understand how people work. Utilise these curious aspects of your personality between the 1st and the 10th. You will be enlightened through deep insights into human nature and improve the quality of your friendships and relationships.

When Mercury, your ruling planet, moves into the career zone after the 6th of February, the same energies can be exploited in your professional arena. This is a chance for you to convey your ideas, no matter how far-fetched they appear at first. Your inventive mind will set the trend amongst your peers.

There is a considerable amount of luck surrounding your talents between the 27th of May and the 26th of June. Making money from your ideas is a distinct possibility under these transits, when Mercury and Jupiter, the planet of luck, bless you with some excellent opportunities. You must be prepared to step outside of your comfort zone to make this a successful trend.

You are competitive this year and after the 9th of September your sporting spirit, debating abilities and intellectual talents can assist you in winning against your competitors. Even if these moments are generally for pleasure, you will have a strong desire to win. Up until the 3rd of October there is an opportunity for you to win money and enjoy the benefits of your speculative tendencies.

I have spoken much about your communications abilities, which you should use to the best possible advantage in your relationships between the 5th and the 15th of December. Love and romance can also benefit from these talents.

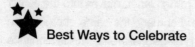 **Best Ways to Celebrate**

Because you're so busy this year, you may wish to take a sabbatical and work on finding ways to relax and calm yourself to the core of your being. This can take place between the 23rd of January and the 5th of February. Make sure you set the trend for the rest of the year by taking adequate rest and enjoying your time alone.

You can extend your celebrations to incorporate people you work with between the 4th and the 20th of March. This is a time when there is a shared interest that can be celebrated, such as the acquisition of a good deal, deadlines that are met or successful negotiations that justify spending some time and money pampering yourself and others.

Once again, after the 14th of April, you take part in a celebratory occasion that could have something to do with being an MC or acting as a key figure on that occasion. In any case, this will also be one of those times of the year when you can thoroughly enjoy yourself and let your hair down.

You can celebrate life when Mercury and Venus influence your Sun sign after the 25th of May. This is also the time of the year when the Sun returns to its birth position for those born under Gemini. You will feel an upswing in energy and generally want to share your good will and joy with others. There will be no particular reason; just the feeling that it's fun to be alive.

You can enjoy a good time on the dance floor, with music and other cultural activities, between the 8th of August and the 23rd of September. This particular cycle activates your creative energies and you will want to celebrate that fact. Celebrate your relationship, love life or marriage during the transit of the Sun in your marital zone after the 22nd of November. Being in a good relationship is reason enough to want to celebrate, isn't it?

KARMA, SPIRITUALITY
AND
EMOTIONAL BALANCE

The most significant planets for your spiritual develop-ment are Mercury, Venus and Uranus. Studying the movement of these planets throughout the coming 12 months will give us a keen insight into those areas of your life that karma will affect most notably. Your past actions, good and bad, will be delivered to you via these planets.

Venus, your love planet and indicator of future karma, enters a favourable place after the 2nd of February. Due to your past actions, demonstrative love and kind words to others, these energies will return to you in full measure. Finding someone who will connect with you on a mental and spiritual level is very likely during this cycle.

This period continues until the end of March, especially around the 29th when Venus and Uranus make a strong contact in your zone of friendships. You'll meet important people who can have a strong bearing on your future destiny. Some of these chance meetings will occur very suddenly and you may not be prepared for the energy and progress that can result from these connections. Be prepared to try new things and to enjoy the good karma that is coming to you.

Some of the effects of these social interactions will be felt throughout the year around the 8th of July, the 15th of August and again around the 17th of October. Your life will be punctuated by good karma, especially in your friendships and more intimate relationships.

Gemini, take care not to overreact between the 8th and the 17th of October. You may want to force things in a relationship and then realise that this is not going to work for you. The process of karma requires you to trust the outcome, be patient and realise that if something is meant to happen, it will happen. Those happenings can culminate at the very end of the year, especially around the 11th of December, when Mercury and Uranus make a vitally positive contact indicating a fulfilment of your desires. This is a very pleasant end to the year and ensures better karma, too.

2013
MONTHLY & DAILY PREDICTIONS

DECISIONS DETERMINE DESTINY.

Frederick Speakman

❊ JANUARY ❊

Monthly Highlight

This is a month of contrasts. You are torn between giving enough attention to yourself and others. Finding a delicate balance between your needs and what others are expecting of you will be a challenge. You are lucky that things could look up for you between the 3rd and the 10th. Romance will be highlighted after the 14th, with some sexual encounters after the 15th. Know when enough is enough.

1 The year kicks off with a focus on travel, promotion, public relations or advertising. This may have something to do with real estate or a property investment that you are keen on.

2 You may act out of fear of lack or poverty and this will affect your thinking. You need to be clear, focused and positive about what you can do. It is not an impossible dilemma.

3 A successful combination of planetary energies ensures success, but you must be prepared to put your emotions aside. If you can do this, you will have a financial coup.

4 Having fun and being creative are the main ingredients to improving your friendships today. Look to some recreation to improve your social standing.

5 Although you feel as if you are in a no man's land, you can find an unexpected emotional opportunity. Balance your inner world with the outer world.

6 You have some health issues to attend to, probably because your daily routine is stressing you out. Your pet, if you have one, may also be a source of concern.

7 A powerful intellectual person may have you on the ropes today. You may think that your reputation depends on winning an argument; it doesn't.

8 It is profitable to travel with the one you love to deepen your relationship. This is a day of intimacy for you.

9 Paperwork could be bothering you. This has to do with shared resources and other tax or banking matters. Don't let it get you down.

10 Your work or career may place you uncomfortably in the limelight. You may need to schedule changes to make yourself available for a public display of your talents.

11 You have a greater need to understand the nature of your personal relationships right now. Don't let emotional sensitivity cloud your judgement.

12 You're interested in understanding your place in the world. You may find some comfort in exploring the world through travel or through higher learning.

13 A new project could find you in a slightly uncomfortable environment, but persist with it and adaptation will be the key to further successes.

14 You could expect a pleasant surprise relating to some of your achievements and be recognised for some of the work you have done.

15 Some of your relatives may be having a difficult time financially. You need to be protective, but don't allow yourself to be used.

16 Health problems caused by inner tension and imbalance need to be addressed. Take care not to exacerbate the situation with poor dietary habits.

17 You feel safe with friends, but may still feel that you are not keeping up with the Joneses. Try not to let envy creep into your relationships.

18 You could feel lost right now. Although a meeting is scheduled, you may prefer to be alone.

19 You need to walk away from friends if the energy is overwhelming. Shape your life according to your current needs.

20 An important discussion could take place, but it could take you into realms of knowledge you hadn't expected. You will be fascinated by intellectual possibilities.

21 You are seeking higher knowledge. Spiritual investigations, religion and even academic studies excite you at the moment.

22 You are feeling anxious. Perhaps the way you look is bothering you. Improve it or forget about it.

23 There may be some minor disappointment in your work. If you are placing too much emphasis on an expectation, you are setting yourself up for a fall.

24 Endings come in all forms, shapes and sizes. A relationship that is no longer necessary may have reached its conclusion. Let it go.

25 Finances are on your mind, but don't project emotional security on what you possess. Develop security from the inside.

26 Today is a day of action and you may find yourself moving around and making changes. Don't do this simply for the sake of change; have an outcome in mind.

27 You may inherit something that at first seems valuable but later becomes a noose around your neck. Discriminate.

28 Security through family connections will be the focus right now. You could be disappointed, however, that your relatives are not admiring your for the good work that you have done.

29 You have clarity of mind, which can help you solve a problem of a financial nature. Friends may also seek your help today.

30 There is a blocked flow of energy, which will result in some lack of success today. Stop fighting with external circumstances and look within to find the solution.

31 The luck you have in overcoming your challenges has everything to do with being creative. Spend some time with children as this will help.

❋ FEBRUARY ❋

Monthly Highlight

Mars activates your career sector today but Neptune, sometimes vague in its effect, means that you are a little confused about how to best proceed. Trust your instincts. You may have to change your work schedule between the 3rd and the 5th. Make sure that your health is up to par to deal with responsibilities that may come your way. Venus, however, is lucky for travel and other cultural or educational pursuits. New opportunities arise after the 8th. Make sure you take advantage of them.

1 You need to assert yourself right now. Planning and constructing your future is in order. Don't shut down emotionally in a relationship. Keep the lines of communication open.

2 Your ambition is at a peak as Mars enters the zone of influence. By all means seek power, but don't abuse it.

3 You have the ability to be recognised in your work and earn more money. Don't stop growing or learning, however, as this is your ticket to an even better future.

4 Don't become complacent in your daily routine. Mix things up so you don't become bored.

5 You could be inundated with work, particularly paperwork. A good filing system and diary are essential to keep you focused and organised.

6 You are focused on others, but don't become too needy. Find the perfect balance between give and take.

7 You need to communicate better at work to increase your successes. Sharing your thoughts today is important.

8 You could feel hurt or embarrassed at work. An awkward emotional situation can be avoided through careful planning and strategising.

9   Paperwork continues to be an issue. You could have more commissions or income, but there are elements of the paperwork that are incomplete.

10   You are full of vitality and going the extra mile will give you the edge over competitors. Control your ego.

11   You have the possibility of either teaching someone or learning something yourself about culture and philosophy. A short trip with someone close is also on the cards.

12   Working behind the scenes is beneficial at the moment. Work quietly to sort out your financial issues or debts.

13   Friendships could be developed under this transit and you will feel safe and supported by your group of friends. But don't become too emotionally attached to someone.

14 Your dreams could be prophetic or problematic. Try to make sense of them by keeping a diary. Soon enough you will understand what they are trying to tell you.

15 Meditation could be an important component of finding balance between yourself and others. Believe it or not, your anxiety could trigger a search for answers that you need right now.

16 You have to make some judgment on a friendship. Be impartial and weigh up the pros and cons in an objective manner.

17 You fear that you may be rejected or that someone is using you. Don't be hurt, impatient or angry; simply look at the situation on its merits.

18 You can now put your best foot forward professionally. Work and social status are on the up and up. Enjoy the benefits of success during this cycle.

19 You have a clear purpose and objective. In your work, you are able to clearly put aside emotional considerations. This means your decisions will be correct.

20 You feel uncomfortable about a project or initiative that falls in your lap. You mustn't accept it if you know you are not going to do the job to the best of your ability.

21 You may acquire something new but will realise that it isn't giving you the satisfaction you initially thought it would. Someone may warn you about this, but you will not listen.

22 There is continued progress in your career and you can expect a few sleepless nights as a result of this. Learn to shut down when the day is over.

23 Contracts, common negotiations and other interactions require clear and purposeful clarity. Be careful that someone is not trying to take advantage of you.

24 If you haven't yet made a decision, it may be best to wait a couple of weeks. All is not lost if you simply wait a little longer.

25 You will enjoy an emotional exchange with someone close to you. If you feel safe with them, this is a perfect way of releasing tension today.

26 You need to have your ego stroked right now, but make sure that the person you are requesting it from is a strong ally and not a competitor. Great success comes with responsibility.

27 Your ideas could make you self-absorbed. Don't overlook another person's needs today.

28 Don't be foolish in love. Check other people's credentials before committing yourself to them. Move slowly in love.

MARCH

 Monthly Highlight

Try to keep a cool head when dealing with friends who are antagonistic. You may be reactive, especially after the 8th. You'll be more socially active, but could spread yourself thin. Make sure you have a backup plan and don't make too many promises to too many people, especially if you know that you are not going to be able to keep them. Some lucky opportunity or gesture of gratitude warms your heart after the 15th.

1 You have an incredible amount of strength and energy and need to direct it properly so you are not frustrated. You need exercise and a healthy outlet to manage these vibrations.

2 Your work routine could be disrupted and you are not able to get a clear schedule in order. This may take consultation to get it right.

3 You need to let go of past hurts and maybe even a circumstance that is holding you back from success. Stop trying to protect a situation that has out-run its usefulness.

4 A new deal can be made as your partnership zone is fully activated. You need discipline and a genuine openness to make things work.

5 You need to take small steps before you can achieve big things. You can be successful with others, but you need team spirit to help you along.

6 Understanding the cycles of life is paramount today. There are emotional undercurrents tied in with financial issues. Clear these up before you move forward.

7 You are chained to a situation of your own making. Breaking free means surrendering or sacrificing something.

8 You need to consciously direct your energies, even if others obstruct you today. Self-confidence is the key to winning others over.

9   If you are divided in your purpose, you will achieve nothing. Family members could be obstructing you and disagreeing with your plans.

10 Your work requires a truce with someone you have considered an adversary. Create harmony in your workplace today.

11 You need to approach someone in a position of authority to make a judgement or ruling. You may be regarded as antagonistic for doing so, but this is necessary.

12 Don't try hard to be popular as this may be your undoing. If you are overlooked, it may be a harmless oversight on the part of someone you know.

13 Go away for a while and make yourself conspicuously absent. This is the quickest way to create value and respect.

14 In your urge to make many friends you could ignore the ones that you already have. Remember to be grateful for what is in your life now.

15 An unexpected emotional event could leave you dazed and confused. You will find solace in charitable work.

16 You could be overwhelmed by others' problems, or perhaps choices that you need to make. You need to prioritise the most important things in your life today.

17 Although you have financial worries, you are still confident enough to move forward and even spend on something you feel you deserve. This is a good strategy, so don't feel guilty about it.

18 Mercury requires you to think more deeply about a course of action than you think is necessary. Postpone your decision until things are clearer.

19 Friends are on the agenda, but you may be emotionally harangued by what's going on in your peer group. Your schedule is subject to changes and upsets. Clarify things beforehand.

20 A reward you are looking forward to may not happen, or it could be less than promised. A breach of trust is likely.

21 Check your junk or spam box in your email. A missing email may have arrived but gone astray.

22 If you treat your clients and co-workers with respect, you will receive repeat business. You have ignored some opportunities that are staring you in the face.

23 Sometimes a disappointment is actually a blessing in disguise. Look at the upside of a let-down. You may be missing some important aspects to the situation.

24 Property matters may have you on the ropes. You are distracted by problems with your family. Step away for a while to catch your breath.

25 Environmental changes will do you the world of good today. You don't have to rush, just plod along even if others are prodding you to do otherwise.

26 Today is a call to action, but that doesn't mean you have to be serious. Keep it all light and breezy.

27 You could embark on some sort of social excursion or be part of a gathering that will make you quite happy today. To gain greater satisfaction from the people involved, don't look at the superficialities.

28 Visitors could end up costing you more than you planned. Finances, as well as emotional expenditure, may leave you feeling a little regretful.

29 Blessings are offered in disguise. A gift you receive may be by way of introduction or delayed response. Don't expect too much.

30 There could be a lack of satisfaction in your personal life due to overwork. Try postponing a couple of meetings to give time to the ones you love.

31 Your success will depend on your initiative and pulling in the right people to assist you in your cause. Don't be an island unto yourself.

Monthly Highlight

The month commences with a high degree of intensity and you need to understand that sometimes you have to let go and not try to control things too much. Work matters will distract you from this after the 6th and some good profitability can be expected as well. Behind-the-scenes activities are spotlighted. Take care of business at home before offering to do too much outside. Health matters may also need to be checked. Don't delay on this.

1   You need to stand back and think about what you are going to do in your work right now. You will probably feel a little lethargic, uninvolved and aloof. This is a gathering stage that requires you to be patient.

2   Sexuality, balance of power and deep emotional transformation are the issues today. You could be upset with someone's lack of response.

3 You feel culturally at odds with your friends or family. Explore alternatives in life.

4 News is bothersome to you because you feel helpless to do anything to help others. Start with your immediate circle of influence, as that is enough.

5 You could be caught off guard or unable to pay some debt or bill. Plan your finances more carefully.

6 Legal matters could go your way. A bureaucratic situation that has been held up could finally be resolved.

7 Solitude and quiet activities are in focus. Staying at home is an attractive option. Health matters are on your agenda. Alternative herbal or homeopathic methods will work.

8 There are opportunities to conduct work on your home or look at the possibility of real estate transactions. You need to carefully calculate the possibilities and your capacity to do this.

9   Don't sweep financial problems under the rug today. It may be easier to cut corners, but this will come back to haunt you in the future.

10   You will be innovative in your work and save time by developing new systems and procedures.

11   Although you are in a position of power, you surprise others by taking a back seat. You need to observe other people's capabilities in order to enhance your own position today.

12   A mystery may be solved, but you need to think outside your normal patterns to come to the right conclusion.

13   You need to be detective-like in working through some emotional issue. Make sure your enquiries are not threatening to others.

14   Your need for emotional autonomy may be met with resistance by someone who is a little possessive. Talk about your feelings to reassure them.

15 You may want to join a group of people who are intellectually like-minded. This will broaden your horizons immensely.

16 Patterns of health continue to undermine your best efforts. You need to take the time to have a check-up to make sure that there is nothing long-term developing.

17 You can earn more money, but you may also want to spend too much. Balance income with expenditure.

18 Time is an essential component of your life and needs to be managed better. Work smart, not just hard, and understand the value of time.

19 You have a need to communicate something to someone but are fearful of the repercussions. If you don't say anything, it might get worse later on.

20 You may feel as if you are losing your sense of identity because you are doing everything for everyone else. Draw a line in the sand and share the burden.

21 A new plan on the home front needs to be a joint effort by everyone involved. You may need to demand support.

22 You need recreation, but everyone is demanding their pound of flesh from you. The magic word is 'no'.

23 You could be on an emotional rollercoaster ride at present, so try to find some balance or, better still, create some space for yourself. Give yourself time.

24 Your emotions may be getting more and more complex, but the solution is to simplify your relationships for the best results. Don't distract yourself with socialising. Solve the problem now.

25 There is an eclipse of the transiting moon right now, and although you feel a little down and out, this is an excellent time to release pent up energies. Work with these energies.

26 You now understand the value of the universal law of karma. Some things that are happening to you relate to your own decision-making in the past. Accept responsibility.

27 You are trying to protect your turf, when in fact you need allies for an initiative you are undertaking. Stop being so territorial.

28 A good venture or journey will be fun but emotionally draining. There needs to be give and take in all relationships. Group dynamics may be a little complicated.

29 You may hear some news that could make you emotionally fretful. You need to work through this and realise that sometimes there is nothing you can do other than send out good vibrations.

30 There is no point in dwelling on the past. Painful events of yesterday cannot be changed. Simply learn from your mistakes.

❁ MAY ❁

Monthly Highlight

You feel opposed in your working life. There is frustration in trying to meet your deadlines when others are trying to obstruct you. After the 4th you may need to request the assistance of an employer or someone who can mediate the situation. Extra-curricular activities can drain you. Between the 20th and the 26th, focus on family matters and slow down the pace.

1 You have feelings of attraction for someone, but may be afraid of where these feelings may take you. Be careful not to indulge too soon.

2 There are emotional pressures that are probably more imagined than real. Postponing discussions may make for more pressure. Don't delay a heart-to-heart.

3 There may be highly charged emotional events that relate to personal viewpoints or even religious or political differences. Sometimes politics and friendship don't mix.

4 Your thoughts may be too caught up in analysing each and every detail of a situation. Trust your intuition instead.

5 You need to control your impulses and endure a situation. You'll need to exercise a conservative approach to win.

6 You could be trying too hard to radically change a situation or someone's perspective. Be convincing without domination.

7 You feel as if you need to be completely unique and individual right now. That's fine, as long as you don't step on other people's toes.

8 You could be experiencing a lack of energy or some strange feelings. If you need to rest, take some time out to get things back to normal.

9 You are probably demanding too much of yourself, as well as others. There may also be some secrets or issues of mistrust in a discussion. This may not be easy to resolve.

10 You feel attractive at the moment and others will be drawn to you. Creating harmony in your environment is your focus.

11 You could be uninformed about a certain person and make decisions based upon faulty perceptions. Seek a third person's advice.

12 You are lucky regarding money and could find yourself the recipient of extra cash. Don't spend all of it as you may need to put some away for a rainy day.

13 You are sensitive in love, but your fantasies are just not in keeping with reality. This extends to your personal relationships or a new-found friend.

14 You are erratic today and may feel as though the means justifies the end. Try to think carefully about the repercussions of your actions today.

15 You have the ability to cooperate with people, even those who have very different viewpoints. Some new type of bonding will bring mutual satisfaction for all.

16 You will be on the road, flitting about here, there and everywhere, and will not have enough time to do the things you really want. Trust your intuition on the things that matter most.

17 Don't let frustration block your ability to connect with someone today. A fear of failure can make things worse.

18 You may forget something important today, like an appointment or some cash. Write yourself a reminder to jog your memory.

19 You could become obsessed with someone and even though this may adversely affect your work, you are unable to change that. Don't display too much emotion.

20 You are wasteful with your money and your feelings. Don't give away too much and compare prices before making a purchase.

21 You may need to deal with a dominating or ruthless female—possibly a woman in your family. A soft diplomatic approach will diffuse the situation.

22 You are confident and optimistic about what you are able to achieve today. If you join a meeting to convince someone of your viewpoint, you will be successful.

23 Don't postpone repaying a debt. There may be interest charges you are overlooking, which means that the amount to be repaid may be slowly getting out of hand.

24 Your desire to socialise at work may interfere with your productivity. Prioritise work and friendship. You mustn't mix them up today.

25 Someone may be too needy for your liking. To keep the peace, you may give more than you feel is fair. Try to talk about your needs.

26 You are impressionable and could believe anything today. Check the facts before signing on the dotted line.

27 Your judgment is better today and speculative ventures could go well on a hunch. You have a keen interest in learning, particularly languages.

28 You are wilful in the way you deal with others and no matter what they say you will hold your ground. Remain flexible in your negotiations.

29 A new project may be difficult to launch, even if you have the financial and emotional support of others. Perhaps your own laziness is the cause of the delay.

30 You have a desire to have fun, but this could be more costly than you anticipate. Look at the alternatives before throwing a lot of cash at the event.

31 Your impulse and desire for self-expression could meet with mishaps. Speed and time are mismatched, which means that you may be rushing to get somewhere. Allow more time in your schedule.

❊ JUNE ❊

Monthly Highlight

You are full of energy and vitality and need to find an appropriate outlet for this. Between the 6th and the 15th, take care when driving, especially if you are running out of time. Mishaps are likely and you can be rather impulsive in your decisions. You continue to make slow but steady progress in your work.

---

1 You may need a stronger ego to deal with some of the characters you're confronted with today. Don't be afraid to assert yourself to get what you want.

---

2 Your generosity may be misplaced at present. Think carefully about what others are trying to get from you before you hand over money or other resources. You could be in error.

---

3 You may feel a sense of abandonment or betrayal. Your generosity continues to be a problem for you.

4 Romance requires you to tread carefully. If you have been single for a while, you may impulsively attempt something that is not in your best interests.

5 You have a depth of feeling, but trusting and sharing these feelings with someone may not be easy. You need someone who is equally as vulnerable to share these deep emotions.

6 You may not be able to control the external circumstances of your life, but internal circumstances are within your means. Work on these to diffuse frustration or resentment.

7 Your idealism will bring you in touch with others of similar ideals. Art, culture and music could be part of the mix.

8 You need to deal with business people in a conservative manner. A pie-in-the-sky attitude may cause lost opportunities. Keep your negotiations grounded in reality.

9   You may over-inflate your sense of self-worth, which could cause others to be let down when they realise the true extent of your abilities. Be humble and honest.

10   The sun is now journeying through your sun sign, which should lift your physical energy levels and give you a boost of self-confidence. Others may look to you for guidance today.

11   A change in plans is unwelcome, but you have no choice or control over it. Have a plan B ready.

12   You can achieve success after a lengthy delay, but your ideals must be grounded in the practical affairs of life. Today is a day of stark contrasts.

13   You may need to contact someone, but you could be completely in the dark as to where they are or how you can make contact. Leave a message and wait for the return call. Don't run yourself into the ground.

14 You need to lock yourself away and do work within your home-sphere. Peace and quiet will afford you moments of deep insight into your problems.

15 Your opinions are requested, but don't expect everyone to agree with you. Clearly articulate your viewpoint and its benefits to others.

16 You are nitpicking when it comes to relationships and setting your standards a little too high. Try not to see the world through rose-colored glasses if you wish for greater success and friendship.

17 You are rash, hot-headed and argumentative today. Blow off a little steam through physical exercise before entering into any sort of debate.

18 You are sexually tense and may possibly take this out on others. This will be more pronounced if you have been spending too much time alone.

19 You are emotional today, but someone may force a rational requirement from you, which you may find difficult to deal with. You may have to tell them that you are unable to discuss the matter right now.

20 You need to control your feelings and this may make you angry. There may be nowhere to turn to other than your higher self.

21 It is as if you have telepathic powers today. Your intuition about someone is correct, so don't go second-guessing yourself.

22 Someone's advances are unwelcome, but as a courtesy you may not let them know about your discomfort. Stop treading on egg shells and speak your mind.

23 You need to consult with a financial planner if you are confused about your financial affairs. Delays in accounting procedures could cause additional confusion.

24 Some of the decisions you have made on an impulse may be snowballing and creating circumstances that are not easy to get out of. You need to grin and bear these consequences for a while longer.

25 You may have no hope of breaking free of a work situation that is depleting you of energy. You need the money but don't appreciate the stress. Focus more clearly on the work rather than what you don't like about it.

26 Your quick responses may help you get out of a tricky situation. You have to be brave in the way you do this, but your instincts will serve you well.

27 You can shape your life in whatever way you choose. Perhaps you want to increase your bank balance or improve your physical vitality. The choice is yours and you have the energy to do it.

28 Taking up a new hobby, particularly an artistic one, will be exciting and bring you in touch with a new social circle.

29 You may impulsively presume someone is wrong, when in fact you are projecting your own feelings on them. Wait to hear their side of the story.

30 Being sentimental could draw you into the past. Remembering the good things is wonderful, but be prepared for reminiscences of the hard times as well. Take the good with the bad.

❋ JULY ❋

Monthly Highlight

Finances take a turn for the better. Jupiter activates your financial zone, with the Sun and Mercury also lending a hand. Additional sources of income are welcome. Save a little extra, however, for a rainy day. Some sudden influx of money may occur in the first week with more steady finances between the 6th and the 10th. Between the 12th and the 18th expect romance to hot up.

1 Your questioning mind and inventive approach to professional problems may invite opposition and even dispute. Try to join with others instead of going against the grain. Team spirit will win out.

2 You can start to enjoy a new cycle of transformation both in your personal relationships and in the way that you pool your resources.

3 Planetary energies provide you further opportunity for financial gain in the world at large. You're able to adapt to your environment and people in your home life far more easily now.

4 An exceedingly lucky set of circumstances is likely to land on your doorstep. New job opportunities or even romantic pursuits will be a thrilling diversion from your usual day-to-day experiences.

5 There will be unsettling energies that are not necessarily negative. You have a strong desire to change things and move outside your normal way of doing things. The urge to purify yourself will extend to such things as health and diet.

6 You could accidentally discover something in your lifestyle or eating habits that has been causing you discomfort or problems. By ferreting out this information you can vastly improve your mental and physical wellbeing.

7 The planets will cause irritation through some stagnation in your professional affairs. If you're working in a situation that has been constricting your creative endeavours, you'll want to break free of these shackles.

8 Intense emotional and romantic affairs pop up, as well as travel associated with these acquaintances. Consider time away from your normal routine.

9 You could be undermining your own best interests due to a fear of speaking your mind. Honesty can be brutal, especially when the people we love do not want to hear what we have to say.

10 You might be thinking of resorting to magic rituals where you perform a ceremony of burning incense, waving candles and uttering incantations of luck and prosperity. It's not that desperate, surely!

11 Your sense of purpose is enshrouded in a mysterious fog and may even vanish. Have you got a purpose or a target? You'd better start thinking about this before you end up at a different destination.

12 The situation in which you feel trapped is only temporary and your pessimism will be replaced by great joy.

13 Timing is everything and you have the chance to gain something that will put your mind at ease. It can act as some sort of correction for debts or losses of the past. On the social scene you may establish a new and better relationship.

14 An unexpected offer from an influential or respected person will surprise and flatter you at the same time. If you choose to accept what's on offer, you stand to gain financially.

15 Although travel may not be to a distant area, your journey will involve considerable amounts of money. You'll be hankering after a shopping spree, social excursion or even a meeting in which you can throw your financial weight around.

16 Shine the spotlight on your finances. Any benefits or extra cash you discover will be short-lived or needlessly wasted on other pursuits.

17 If you feel the tension mounting, it means you've taken on too much. Know when enough is enough and say 'no' to that additional chore or extra responsibility that is going to weigh you down.

18 Seeking answers from partners and friends will be easy under the current influences. By the same token, be careful, as seeking answers may be a lot easier than learning the truth.

19 You could have a difficult time distinguishing between lust and love. If you're in a committed relationship, it will be confusing. This usually signals an identity crisis.

20 This is a roller-coaster period in your life. While enjoying good social situations and acceptance, you still feel as though this is not enough.

21 You will be attracted to extravagance and goods that may not be essential for the smooth functioning of your life. Be careful not to be duped by slick, fast-talking salespeople.

22 New friendships arise. You certainly want to develop new associations, but are equally tied to the old way of doing things. This will cause you irritation, and a little fear too, as you realise that growth means letting go.

23 Harmonious relationships with co-workers stimulate others to involve you in some of their activities. Long-distance communications with friends or colleagues will also bolster your confidence.

24 You could become rather dissatisfied with the level and quality of your work. Don't be too hard on yourself.

25 Be clear on the standards you set for yourself. Any misgivings or frustrations you've held in your heart must be vented as soon as possible to avoid the serious undermining of your partnerships in the coming months.

26 You feel burdened by your past and this could inhibit the way you interact with others. Dragging unsavoury experiences into the present and superimposing them onto new relationships is a cocktail for failure.

27 You'll be stimulated by relationships and inspired to try something far more unusual than you normally would. Someone important to your future could attract your attention and offer you some new experiences.

28 Don't become depressed over trifling matters. If you do, you'll miss the bigger picture. In any endeavour, relationship or path of activity, take it for granted that you're going to have obstructions and that the odd thing can go off beam.

29 There's nothing worse than a regretful romantic experience. You shouldn't race to the bedroom in any new encounter. It's far better to get more background on the person before you venture into 'hot-n-spicy' territory.

30 Passionate desires can overwhelm you, so you need to have someone to share them with. Fortune favours the brave, not only financially but in matters of the heart. Be a little more aggressive in your relationships.

31 Financial responsibilities can be a little uncomfortable for you. Break debts or fiscal responsibilities into bite-size morsels so you can digest them individually.

AUGUST

Monthly Highlight

You have big plans this month but may not be aware that you need greater resources and skills than you currently have. Between the 4th and the 8th is a good time to investigate educational programs to improve your abilities on the work front. You are happy at home as Venus softens your social appetites. Family affairs prosper.

1 You need to beef up your financial reserves. The bucket of fiscal prudence has a few holes in it and you need to block them up so you don't waste your hard-earned money. Treat yourself and others, if you have to, but don't buy the most expensive dish on the menu.

2 There's a danger of financial loss, theft or simply forgetfulness that results in the misplacing of valuables.

3 Trying to establish what's truly good or bad for you won't be easy. You're prepared to take a punt, and this doesn't necessarily relate to the financial aspects of your life.

4 You can afford to be somewhat zany and this will give you enough charm and charisma to win over people's hearts. In fact, a little bit of wackiness will bring you good fortune.

5 You're highly excitable and this has a lot to do with the fact that you are spreading your wings and flying—in the mental sense, at least. Expect good news regarding a financial matter or legal issue.

6 Share some time with friends in a sporting arena. Physical activity, where you are an active participant or you have the opportunity to enjoy the company of others, is likely.

7 You'll start to feel a lot of power building up in your life. This is one of the best times of the year, and the next month or two will give you the chance to strut your stuff on the stage of life.

8 Let your fantasies run wild. Your sensitivity will be well received by a lover or friend. You have a desire to try new things and to push your love to the limits.

9 The health of a friend or loved one may cause some worry. You may have to shoulder this additional responsibility and cop it on the chin. Balancing your work, social and compassionate obligations will require some careful manoeuvring on your part.

10 Parties and other social endeavours will be successful. Standing out from the crowd will be more important now. Anything you can do to appear more flamboyant will be desirable.

11 Your finances improve. Independent business owners will see an upswing in their overall profitability. If you run a family business, other members of your clan are more likely to appreciate your hard work and lend a hand.

12 This is a time for you to shine. Your professional activities, reputation and financial position are all spotlighted. It's also a great time to express yourself with authority.

13 Promotions, new jobs and other work opportunities are at their peak during this time.

14 You are motivated to achieve more in your personal relationships. The other party must now reciprocate!

15 You may have to divide your attention and loyalties on the home front—much to the dismay of loved ones. You could feel as though you are giving equal time to relatives and work, but the perceived value by others is different. Talk about what's expected of you.

16 Some favourable news in a relationship will give you cause for jubilation. If you've felt negative about a love affair, you may need to change your viewpoint.

17 If you've been hiding, it's time to become more outgoing. Getting out and about and moving outside your home turf will expand your mind and give you a taste of different cultures and views.

18 Before passing judgment on a lover or partner, exhaust all avenues of investigation. You'll be quick to jump to conclusions as your mind races from one topic to another.

19 You're likely to be impulsive while getting tedious matters out of the way. In doing so, you will overlook important facts that could be your undoing. Attention to detail is necessary.

20 Continue to monitor your finances. The strong focus on shared resources will require diligence and concentrated effort on your part. Compare financial plans before making decisions.

21 Providing help for those in need will require some extra time on your part. You want a diversionary tactic, so this could work out quite well for everyone involved.

22 Mapping out your destiny is not easy when you feel that fate is out of your control. But you can at least create some guidelines and time frames from which to work and minimise the so-called X-factor.

23 Avoid putting yourself into risky emotional situations unless you're ready to deal with feelings. You can go to extremes. On the other hand, you may find that a flexible attitude will give you great insight into your inner workings.

24 You could push someone's mind to the limit. You may also be attempting some mental gymnastics that are possibly out of character. This could backfire if you're trying to resolve any deep-seated issues.

25 Contracts bring more security into your life. This will have to do with leases, rental apartments or even work-related odds and ends. Make sure you have the right advice before signing on the dotted line.

26 Your interests in beauty, culture and the arts are strong. You need to find someone who shares your desire for these more refined activities.

27 Taking up a new hobby or craft is not a bad idea. You will become very idealistic and start a more serious and rigorous discipline of creative visualisation.

28 The Sun spotlights your need to associate with organisations, groups or clubs. If you've been lax and not had the time to reinstate your membership, now is the time to do so.

29 Your expectations in love will not reach the heights you anticipate. Be realistic about what your partner can do. By being more empathetic, you're more likely to have your needs met as well.

30 Uncomfortable meetings or dealing with people who you don't click with are unavoidable. You'll have to call a spade a spade to tie up a business deal or get to the bottom of an issue.

31 A rekindling of your friendship with friends and social acquaintances will be exciting and timely. This also ties in with your connection with the past and reinvigorating some of your long-forgotten friendships.

SEPTEMBER

Monthly Highlight

You are on the move this month and can expect a great deal of communication. Between the 3rd and the 8th you may have a particularly hectic schedule. Eat well and spend a little more time resting. Mars is notorious for mishaps, so take your time and be careful when operating electrical or mechanical devices.

1 You may have to say 'yes' to your partner, even if you're feeling a little stressed and dominated by them. By disagreeing, you'll make a rod for your own back. Being agreeable is the way out.

2 Your self-assurance is really high and you are firing on all cylinders. Make the best of what you've got. You can use this time creatively, especially with partnerships.

3 Amidst your dynamic activities, the planets continue to whip up a storm in your life. Your mind is oscillating between the not-so-distant past and the future to give you relief from the present.

4 You don't feel very creative, but there are other ways in which you can express your gifts. Cooking, decorating your home and doing other handicrafts are ways for you to escape the humdrum routine.

5 You're likely to be saying less and meaning more today. Talk is cheap but ideas are dear, so concentrate on what's important and eliminate what isn't.

6 If your sleeping patterns are disturbed, you must deal with the root of the problem or this will affect your work. Pruning will only work temporarily. Travel will also become a far greater focus over these coming months.

7 Big steps in the expansion of your ideas are possible. It is not the right moment for drastic changes, but for capitalising in the potential of directions already taken.

8 You probably want to be left alone. The planets create less desire to impress than usual. This is probably just as well. There will be a few additional work responsibilities.

9 An unusual sense of independence will develop in you. It's during these types of planetary cycles that you are likely to realise your own self-worth and make some radical changes in your personal and professional life.

10 You need to use your creative imagination to determine your future, especially if where you are at is not where you would ideally like to be.

11 You may be underpaid and overworked and fearful of changing the status quo due to issues of financial security, but it could be time for you to actively seek new work.

12 Excellent aspects for transmitting your ideas, writing letters and attending job interviews. You'll make a great impact at meetings.

13 You need to scrutinise people more carefully. With financial transactions, remain aware and keep your mind on what you're doing.

14 Your thinking will not be as open as you think it is and others may not be receptive to your ideas. You will also be worried about some recurring trifling matters.

15 Unless you try something, you're never going to know. Even if the outcome is not favourable, at least you can say you gave it a shot.

16 Family affairs run slowly and you could decide to pick up the pace. If you've been complacent, others will take advantage of you. Exercise power over others and you'll be surprised at the results you get.

17 Extending yourself to assist others in your work may be hard at first, but you'll get top marks for taking the time to be compassionate.

18 You will be feeling in harmony with yourself and finding satisfaction in the personal sphere of your life. This has ramifications for your love life and you may enter a slightly more independent phase.

19 Romance is likely to be favourable so don't push yourself to any unnecessary limits by spending excessively on gifts or attire to win favour. Be cool, be yourself, and all will go well.

20 A new introduction could jolt you out of your lethargy and introspection and make you seriously consider a rendezvous, dinner or other special outing.

21 You may desire a new life elsewhere, so this cycle is connected with endings, legal matters and possibly moving or purchasing a new home.

22 It's time for a review of taxes, insurance and other fees that are tied in with property and family matters. Distributing the costs equitably could be a topic of discussion.

23 Two camps may emerge in your family life. Old versus young? Radical versus conventional? Either way, there'll be a difference of opinion on certain matters in your domestic sphere.

24 Disturbing changes in your home environment or neighbourhood could cause you to overreact. It's likely that you need to reinvest some time in your local affairs.

25 A family reunion is an ideal way to bring relatives together. If there's been tension on the home front, it's time to reconnect and get back to the good old days. Avoid serious topics to smooth the situation over.

26 The secret to taking your love life to the next level is being sensitive and not playing a game of one-upmanship.

27 You need to make some last minute changes to your family's routine to help it fit in with other activities on your agenda. Unfortunately, you will have to bear some friction from others who have alternative plans.

28 Your creativity is at a high point but you must determine how to properly direct those energies.

29 Reach out to the public and let yourself shine. You are able to do your best at the moment and people will recognise your talents.

30 You'll probably realise that celibacy is not for you. However, moments of contemplation and time out can be quite balancing for you right now.

❋ OCTOBER ❋

Monthly Highlight

You have several choices in your workplace this month and may even think of leaving. The Moon and Mars together may cause you to be rash, so don't do things hastily. Investigate your options, especially after the 10th. Sometime after the 14th, a friend may suddenly inspire you with the correct course of action.

1 You can have your way, but you don't necessarily have to fight for it. Gentle persuasion will work wonders and you will not need to labour to achieve the goal.

2 After a whole lot of stop-and-start decision-making, you can finally make headway on some travel plans. Choose travel companions wisely.

3   You have to work behind the scenes to break new ground and this will involve being more guarded about your intentions. Be careful who you share your plans with.

4   Cold hard facts are not available and others probably won't believe you. This is your intuition working at its best, and whatever it's telling you about someone ought to be heeded.

5   Don't be afraid to put the screws on others who are dragging their feet and expecting you to do the majority of the work. If team members are not pulling their weight, you'll have to pressure them.

6   You'll feel far more dynamic, which will give a boost to different aspects of your life. Your work and reputation are back on track. Make those important meetings and create win-win circumstances for all concerned.

7   You will score a considerable win or increase in finance and reputation, which allows you the luxury of slowing your pace and enjoying the fruits of your hard work.

8 You must resist the temptation of overloading yourself with work. Self-worth and looking after your own needs are the secret to your growth today.

9 The key word today is charm. By switching it on, you'll find greater success that if you apply your usual mental gymnastics.

10 Wonderful news can reinvigorate your ambitious urges. The success of a sibling or neighbour can be the cause of celebration or partying.

11 Your own emotions will be heightened, and for those who are unable to connect with their deeper emotional self, this is a time when it will happen.

12 You will have to turn up the heat on a lover. Lethargy, apathy and other negative emotions will irritate you. You can see the solution but they are stuck in a rut.

13 You can sense a strong psychic bond with a romantic possibility. Communications will be strong but verbalising these feelings will not be easy.

14 Power struggles in your romantic life could knock the edge off what you ordinarily consider to be a good thing. You're over-emotional and reacting to things you shouldn't.

15 If you have your heart set upon some romantic destination, don't forget to make the booking and allocate appropriate time.

16 What goes around comes around. A lot of your emotional and romantic output is coming back and you'll be surprised at the demonstrative nature of those nearest and dearest to you.

17 You are giving off the right signals but not getting the response and affection you'd like. Maybe you are being a little too demanding at this point in time. Try to exercise a little compassion.

18 You'll be feeling either intuitive, spiritual or like someone in a mystery thriller. You'll need to look at things from a completely different dimension if you're going to understand anything at all.

19 You mustn't let your arrogance get in the way of seeking the opinion or advice of someone more capable than you. Trust is the key element.

20 You'll feel as though you've been left out of an occasion, social engagement or other work activity. Don't be afraid to subtly apply pressure to those who have overlooked you.

21 You have a sneaking suspicion about someone's character but find yourself between a rock and a hard place when it comes to sharing this information with anyone else.

22 Much of your focus is on financial matters. Taking solid advice from advisors or financial planners will pay off if you give appropriate attention to these matters throughout the month.

23 Don't make decisions about your financial future on a whim or uninformed guesswork. You could lose money on that front. Speculations should also be avoided.

24 It's time for you to assert yourself rather than accept an error that could create turmoil in your mind.

25 Your sense of duty and responsibility will overpower the more emotional and romantic elements of your relationship. Not being supported in your creative endeavours could make things seem a little bleak at the moment.

26 Some news will bring you into the public eye or make you join with new people to coordinate your efforts towards a single goal.

27 You have to synchronise your efforts with family members. A strong focus on finances means that a divided household brings material problems.

28 A speedy getaway can tie in with a creative enterprise. Get back in touch with those you've had little time for.

29 You can tie up any legal or bureaucratic issues through some unconventional but strategic moves. If your legal counsel has been less than satisfactory, opt for someone with a fresher approach.

30 Increased income is of no use if you spend it as quickly as you earn it. Start putting aside some of those extra dollars for a rainy day.

31 Get your phone calls and emails out of the way early. You'll achieve a lot in a short span of time and rewards will be forthcoming. The early bird catches the worm.

☀ NOVEMBER ☀

Monthly Highlight

You are full of love this month but may also be a little obsessive. The fanatical energies of Pluto need to be managed well, otherwise they could destroy you. Try to find activities to give your compulsive emotions a positive turn, especially between the 6th and the 15th. You may want to do your work on home turf. This will free up your time substantially for more leisure activities.

1   Good luck comes in threes so be on the lookout for those omens. As the day wears on, each successive omen could herald better things.

2   You will want an impromptu outing but will find yourself out of your depth when the company you fall into becomes a tad strange. It's not a bad idea to get a preview from friends as to who will be a part of the action.

3 The insinuation that you're not completely honest could have you seeing red. This could come in the form of innuendo from someone you thought better of.

4 You feel apprehensive about new information that challenges you. You can only make sense of it if you don't operate from a base of panic.

5 You'll feel that someone doesn't make as much effort as you and isn't committed to the friendship. You are overlooking some subtle and important contributions they made in the past.

6 You mustn't take your daily routine for granted as everything around you is constantly changing. Becoming stuck in a way of doing things can fall apart.

7 You have to make time to reorganise your habits and reinvent your itinerary. You may look to others whom you feel are more capable at this, but ultimately this is a do-it-yourself issue.

8   You have the capacity to overcome great odds. On the negative side, you will be controlling and find it hard to separate the desire for achievement from control issues. This will be your core focus at the end of the month.

9   An important day for connecting with a person or group of people who can help you advance in the right direction economically.

10   You will have to sit on the fence for a little longer until you feel confident that a new friendship is something far deeper.

11   New work opportunities through friends are favourable. Upping the ante on your résumé and getting your references in order will help you in any job seeking.

12   Try to stay a little more grounded—and that means dealing with some overwhelming feelings that are the result of sexuality and deeper emotions.

13 You may discover a bond with someone. Developing a friendship will inspire you.

14 You may be excited and obsessive about relationships right now. Try to maintain a level-headed view about things without getting carried away.

15 You have the power to heal someone. You need to reassure them that they are feeling well before they believe it. You'll be surprised at your capacity to remove ill feelings.

16 You need to relax, but not in a busy place. It's a time for bringing together friends in a quiet environment and reminiscing about the good times.

17 You may feel that a new responsibility or work achievement may clash with the needs of someone close. Don't worry—the two will converge in their own good time.

18 Today you may not be open in your dealings with others, so to try to avoid big bad egos. You want to keep your cards close to your chest. You may also act passive-aggressively.

19 You'll have to tap into your inner forces to advance today. Don't become obsessive about self-interests. It may separate you from your intimate relationships.

20 Today you may feel hurt and unappreciated. This may bring you an awareness of your own shortfalls, which can help you advance and rise above a sense of neediness.

21 Take time out to listen to conventional wisdom as you may be reckless and fiery today. Practical advice may help you channel your energies into productive pursuits.

22 Mould your surroundings and make use of plants, fragrances, candles and other artifacts to simulate faraway places. Tranquility will come from your imagination.

23 You may be prone to romantic extremism and reject 'normal' friendships, regardless of their intrinsic value. Learn to compromise or you may get others' backs up.

24 You may invite trouble in your family circle by not agreeing with a 'good' idea. You'll feel bored with tradition so do your own thing and avoid the hassle.

25 Your mouth may be on automatic pilot. Don't finish other people's sentences for them! Take care of dental issues.

26 Today you can channel your moods and energy to provide useful suggestions to loved ones. Do this subtly and you will gain benefits in a roundabout way.

27 A troublesome issue is repeating in your mind like a broken record. Today's lesson is to move your mind into a thought-free state.

28 Don't deny spontaneity in your personality. You can be absorbed in doing the job right and forget the greater power of who you are. Be aware.

29 Recent confusion in your relationships gives way to an enlightened view. A current friendship was misunderstood as a result of your overly idealistic standards.

30 You can either get caught up in the same old rigmarole with family members, or try a different approach. A bit of reverse psychology goes a long way!

Monthly Highlight

You could feel dull and uninspired at work. The challenge is to find creative ways to make life interesting. Meeting new people can help and this can happen after the 11th. You could overwhelm yourself by taking on too many responsibilities for the Christmas break. Choose your entertainment and social circle carefully. The 25th until the 28th is a very satisfactory period.

1   You're feeling confident, but Mercury could be tempting you to feel down about some of your less than desirable character traits. Be positive!

2   You think you've resolved an issue with someone who tampered with your emotions. Retrace your mental steps to discover why a relationship ended the way it did.

3 Responsibility is weighing heavily upon you. In the next two days, you will need to resolve some issues from elder members of your family or superiors at work.

4 Shifting circumstances with family members require an agile mind. Maintain your personal views and individual outlook without unsettling others.

5 Confronting an issue will be distasteful for both the teller of the story and the one listening, but only the truth will clear up these issues once and for all.

6 This is an important transition where you determine the value of your relationships in every area of your life. Letting go may be hard, but it is essential for improving yourself and your life generally.

7 Try not to be sidetracked by what everyone else is doing and focus on what you have to create. To ensure all your personal needs are satisfied, eat before you start!

8 If a promise has been broken, you can bet that you didn't trust your instincts, or that you applied too much pressure. Take time out and reassess.

9 Someone who's been a large part of your life could offer you something you've been longing for. It will come as a surprise.

10 Consider what you are happy with before you tackle what you're not happy with! The pressure of holding an event has taken its toll. Try to take it in your stride.

11 Today may involve wiping someone's tears away. You've forgotten something important or left things wide open for doubt. The black cloud will lift quickly.

12 Let everyday worries pass you by and welcome the amazing fun and laughter that could be offered to you from unexpected sources today. It's time to take up a new hobby.

13 You'll struggle with an unexpected decision someone makes concerning a family feud. Accept that this person does not have to consult you first.

14 There's a big step for you to take right now, so weigh up all the options. A gamble of sorts is necessary even if the stakes are high.

15 If you prefer to do things in a way that you find efficient, talk to your boss/partner and see if your needs can be accommodated without affecting the job.

16 Due to the fact that work and your social life may overlap, you need to be strong in drawing the line between business and pleasure. No shop talk!

17 Go on the offensive today. Grab Cupid by the neck and get him to bring you the one you love. Don't wait around wondering whether his arrows are a hit-and-miss affair.

2013: MONTHLY & DAILY PREDICTIONS | 195

18 It seems there are far more messages on your answering machine than usual. Getting back to everyone is time-consuming but also fun. You can feel your popularity growing.

19 Remain aware to what the Universe is saying to you. A friend will be instrumental in the outcome of these omens and the corresponding events during these few days.

20 A third party may need to verify your credentials. This is not going to help the friendship, but it's necessary.

21 A friend has some gossip for you. This could make you mentally restless and even a bit nervous.

22 Your work at the moment can be challenging but also inspiring. Ask yourself where to direct the majority of your efforts. There may be several different directions that all seem appealing. Making choices is difficult but essential if you are to effectively use your talents.

23 You are forced to adapt to the person you love or a partner you wish to keep. You may think that their demands are over-the-top, but these changes are for your personal growth and greater welfare.

24 If you have a heavy workload, it's best to stay away from too much socialising otherwise you'll find yourself with twice as much work tomorrow. Don't make any apologies for spending time alone today.

25 A problem with an older male, probably your father or a hard-nosed employer, will not be easy to solve at this time. You could feel as if you are being singled out amongst your peers.

26 In your greater efforts to save money and not be frivolous, you might start to begrudge the fact that you don't have as good a lifestyle as others.

27 A radical and unexpected change in your domestic situation may cause you some concerns. Perhaps you were the one who instigated the overhaul, facelift or improvement that has cost you more than you expected.

28 If you go on a blind date or have recently met someone who is interested in you, you mustn't let your nerves get the better of you. Remain calm, cool and collected in the way you express yourself.

29 Working on your negotiation skills seems to be a theme right now and it will work wonders for both your financial position and relationships, particularly if you feel you have been under someone's thumb.

30 You have to get your schedule in order if you are to be successful in the coming months. This means sacrificing some of the little pleasures in life.

31 If you have been there for a friend in need, you may now have to deal with the fact that you have minimised their responsibility in the issue.

2013
ASTRONUMEROLOGY

WE'RE DROWNING IN
INFORMATION AND STARVING
FOR KNOWLEDGE.

Rutherford D. Rogers

THE POWER BEHIND YOUR NAME

Did you know that your name actually resonates at a certain frequency, a vibration that is unique to you? To find out what this vibration is, and how it affects you and your destiny, you simply add the numbers of your name to reveal which planet is governing you. This is an ancient form of numerology based upon the Chaldean system in which each number is assigned a planetary vibration. Take a look at the chart below to see how each alphabetical letter is connected to a planetary energy.

AIJQY	=	1	**Sun**
BKR	=	2	**Moon**
CGLS	=	3	**Jupiter**
DMT	=	4	**Uranus**
EHNX	=	5	**Mercury**
UVW	=	6	**Venus**
OZ	=	7	**Neptune**
FP	=	8	**Saturn**
—	=	9	**Mars**

Note: The number 9 is not allotted a letter because it is a mysterious vibration and considered 'unknowable'.

Once the numbers have been added together, they result in a number which is associated with a planet that rules your name and personal affairs.

It is no accident that many famous actors, writers and musicians have modified their names. They use these name changes to attract luck and good fortune, which can be facilitated by using the energies of a friendlier planet. Try experimenting with the table and see how new names affect you. It's so much fun and may even attract greater love, wealth and worldly success!

By studying the following example, you too can work out the power of your name. If your name is Andrew Brown, calculate the ruling planet by correlating each letter to a number in the table, like this:

A	N	D	R	E	W		B	R	O	W	N
1	5	4	2	5	6		2	2	7	6	5

And then add the numbers like this:

$1 + 5 + 4 + 2 + 5 + 6 + 2 + 2 + 7 + 6 + 5 =$ **45**

Then add $4 + 5 =$ **9**

The ruling number of Andrew Brown's name is 9, which is ruled by Mars. (See how the nine can now be used?) Now study the Name-Number Table to reveal the power of your name. The numbers 4 and 5 will play a secondary role in Andrew's character and destiny, so in this case you would also study the effects of Uranus (4) and Mercury (5).

Your Name Number	Ruling Planet	Name Characteristics
1	Sun	Beautiful character. Able to sway people with their charm. Physically active. They enjoy sports and other competitive activities. Many friends and rich and wealthy well-wishers. Excellent connections in government circles and with political individuals. Makes a wonderful friend. Can be loyal but stubborn.
2	Moon	Soft, receptive and emotional by nature. Extreme change of moods. Highly sensitive and psychic. Curious nature, kind-hearted and creative in many areas. Strong love of family and friends. Prefers night to day. Women have a strong karmic influence on them.

Your Name Number	Ruling Planet	Name Characteristics
3	Jupiter	Strong philosophical nature. Supreme optimist but at times opportunistic, which is unnecessary because a great deal of luck is associated with Jupiter. Great sense of timing. Expansive and generous nature that may be wasteful at times. Travel will bring them many interesting experiences.
4	Uranus	Unusual character with an erratic nature. Unusual likes and dislikes. Many unexpected experiences, ups and downs and interesting but short-lived relationships. May become bored easily and needs to plan more carefully for a stable life.
5	Mercury	Master communicator. A love of change and variety which may lead to an ever-shifting pattern of life without stability. Always young at heart, playful and attractive to all. Attracted to the written and spoken word. Quick witted.

Your Name Number	Ruling Planet	Name Characteristics
6	Venus	Seductive and delightful personality. Gracious and social by nature. Eye-catching personality with a variety of friends. Expert in bedroom arts and also able to make money through social activities. Music, art and other aesthetic activities take pride of place in life. Strong family ties that need to be carefully balanced with career appetites.
7	Neptune	One of the most spiritual numbers, which indicates a psychic and self-sacrificing nature. Unconditional in love and able to develop the most altruistic character. Prophetic, a dreamer, but sometimes victimised by the very people they wish to help. Can be a romantic idealist.

Your Name Number	Ruling Planet	Name Characteristics
8	Saturn	An excessively hard worker, sometimes overly preoccupied by money and security. Great powers of concentration. Will usually work long and hard to achieve ambitions. Slow in giving trust and demands perfection in all areas of life. Sometimes overly serious, but a loyal character.
9	Mars	Immense stamina and recuperative powers. Highly physical and sexual individual. Often steamrolls others, but means well. Combative, competitive, arrogant and playful. Injury-prone. Protects family and is extremely loyal to all he or she considers important. Great success through sheer effort.

YOUR PLANETARY
⚜ RULER ⚜

Astrology and numerology are very closely aligned. Each planet rules over a number between 1 and 9. Both your name and your birth date are ruled by planetary energies. Here are the planets and their ruling numbers:

1   **Sun**

2   **Moon**

3   **Jupiter**

4   **Uranus**

5   **Mercury**

6   **Venus**

7   **Neptune**

8   **Saturn**

9   **Mars**

To find out which planet will control the coming year for you, simply add the numbers of your birth date and the year in question. Here is an example:

If you were born on 12 November, add the numerals 1 and 2 (12, your day of birth) and 1 and 1 (11, your month of birth) to the year in question, in this case 2013 (current year), like this:

Add 1 + 2 + 1 + 1 + 2 + 0 + 1 + 3   =   **11**

1 + 1   =   **2**

The planet ruling your individual karma for 2013 will be the Moon because this planet rules the number 2.

YOUR PLANETARY
FORECAST

You can even take your ruling name number, as shown above, and add it to the year in question to throw more light on your coming personal affairs, like this:

A N D R E W B R O W N =   9

Year coming   =   2013

Add 9 + 2 + 0 + 1 + 3   =   15

Add 1 + 5   =   6

This is the ruling year number using your name number as a basis. You would then study the influence of Venus (6) for 2013. Good luck!

Trends for Your Planetary Number in 2013

Year Number	Ruling Planet	Results Throughout the Coming Year
1	Sun	

Overview

The commencement of a new cycle: a year full of accomplishments, increased reputation, brand new plans and projects. New responsibilities, success and strong physical vitality. Health should improve and illnesses will be healed. If you have ailments, this is the time to improve your physical wellbeing—recovery will be certain.

Love and Pleasure

A lucky year for love. Credit connection with children. Family life is in focus. Music, art and creative expression will be fulfilling. New romantic opportunities.

Work

Minimal effort for maximum luck. Extra money and exciting professional opportunities. Positive new changes result in promotion and pay rises.

Improving Your Luck

Luck is plentiful, particularly in July and August. The 1st, 8th, 15th and 22nd hours of Sundays are lucky.

Your lucky numbers are 1, 10, 19 and 28.

Year Number	Ruling Planet	Results Throughout the Coming Year
2	Moon	

Overview

Reconnection with your emotions and past. Excellent for relationships with family members. Moodiness may become a problem. Sleeping patterns will be affected.

Love and Pleasure

Home, family life and relationships are in focus this year. Relationships improve through self-effort and greater communication. Change of residence, renovations and interior decoration bring satisfaction. Increased psychic sensitivity.

Work

Emotional in work. Home career, or hobby from a domestic base, will bring greater income opportunities. Females will be more prominent in your work.

Improving Your Luck

July will fulfil some of your dreams. Monday will be lucky with the 1st, 8th, 15th and 22nd hours being particularly fortunate. Pay special attention to the New and Full Moons in 2013.

Your lucky numbers include 2, 11, 20, 29 and 38.

Year Number	Ruling Planet	Results Throughout the Coming Year
3	Jupiter	

Overview

A lucky year for you. Exciting opportunities will expand your horizons. Good fortune financially. Travels and increased popularity. A happy year. Your spiritual inclinations will grow and you will also want to explore the world. Travel is on the cards.

Love and Pleasure

You feel confident about romance during this cycle. You may meet someone during busy activity or while travelling. This is a good opportunity to deepen your love for your partner.

Work

Fortunate for new opportunities and success. Employers are more accommodating and open to your creative expression. Extra money. New job promotions are possible.

Improving Your Luck

Remain realistic, get more sleep and don't expect too much from your efforts. Planning is necessary for better luck. The 1st, 8th, 15th and 24th hours of Thursdays are spiritually very lucky for you.

Your lucky numbers are 3, 12, 21, and 30. March and December are lucky months. 2013 will bring you some unexpected surprises.

Year Number	Ruling Planet	Results Throughout the Coming Year
4	Uranus	

Overview

Don't take things for granted during this cycle as changes may occur when you least expect them. Unexpected twists and turns of fate. Possibility of having to begin all over again. Progressive attitude may bring many unusual and uplifting experiences.

Love and pleasure

Guard against dissatisfaction in relationships. You require plenty of freedom and experimentation. Love may take you by surprise. You could meet someone when you least expect it, but the relationship may turn out to be tumultuous.

Work

Unusual and modern lines of work are likely in the coming year and you need to be open to new ideas to enhance your career prospects. Working with technological apparatus, software and other online tools will be of interest to you. Try not to overwork and find ways to reduce your stress levels.

Year Number	Ruling Planet	Results Throughout the Coming Year

Improving your luck

Temperance is your keyword in the coming 12 months. Be patient and do not rush things. Slow your pace this year as impulse will only lead to errors and missed opportunities. Exercise greater patience in all matters. Steady investments are lucky.

The 1st, 8th, 15th and 20th hours of any Saturday will be very lucky for you in 2013.

Your lucky numbers are 4, 13, 22 and 31.

Year Number	Ruling Planet	Results Throughout the Coming Year
5	Mercury	

Overview

You are moving so quickly that things appear to be in fast-forward mode. You need to pace yourself, even if your imagination and communication skills are at a peak. New ideas will fascinate you and life will seem full of opportunities.

Intellectual activities and communications increase. Your imagination is powerful. New and exciting ideas will bring success and personal satisfaction.

Love and Pleasure

Relationships take on a more playful air in 2013. You must be adaptable to keep pace with your family members and your own schedule. Love affairs may be confusing as you could become indecisive. Try to accept your spouse or partner for who they are. You may become critical. Learn to curb your impulse to find fault.

Work

Your innovative ideas put you ahead of your work peers. You will meet many people and may also develop an interest in commerce and finance. You will want to trade and increase profitability in your business.

Year Number	Ruling Planet	Results Throughout the Coming Year

You can achieve a senior position if you are prepared to assume additional responsibilities. Don't do too much. Speed, efficiency and capability are your keywords this year. Don't be impulsive in making a career change. Travel is also on your agenda.

Improving Your Luck

Write down your ideas, research topics more thoroughly, and communicate your enthusiasm through meetings. This will afford you much more luck. Stick to one idea.

The 1st, 8th, 15th and 20th hours of Wednesday are luckiest, so schedule your meetings and other important social engagements at these times.

Your lucky numbers are 5, 14, 23 and 32.

Year Number	Ruling Planet	Results Throughout the Coming Year
6	Venus	

Overview

2013 will be an important year for romance and new relationships. You will be sensual as well as sexually self-indulgent. Your family affairs will take precedence over other aspects of your life. You may want to work with the one you love. Money should be plentiful, but only if you reduce your overheads and unnecessary expenses.

Love and Pleasure

Your keyword in the next 12 months is romance. An existing romance is deepened now. You may meet someone new who can help you develop greater self-esteem. You will take on a new look. Put your best foot forward. Engagement, or even marriage, is quite possible. Increase in social responsibilities. Moderate your excessive tendencies.

Work

Your protective instincts and desire for greater future security will dominate your working life. You will be finding ways to cut back costs and save more money. Combining your professional and domestic life is also likely. Working from home may be preferable.

Year Number	Ruling Planet	Results Throughout the Coming Year

Improving Your Luck

Work and success are dependent on your creative and positive mental attitude. Eliminate bad habits and personality tendencies that can obstruct you. Balance spiritual and financial needs.

The 1st, 8th, 15th and 20th hours on Fridays are extremely lucky for you this year and new opportunities can arise when you least expect it.

The numbers 6, 15, 24 and 33 will generally increase your luck.

Year Number	Ruling Planet	Results Throughout the Coming Year
7	Neptune	

Overview

This is an intuitive and spiritually karmic year. Your life goals become more focused, but you need to rely on your inner resources to get you across the line. You need to be careful of people who might use you this year. Don't be too trusting.

Love and Pleasure

You may meet someone who is your spiritual soul mate this year. Your love is idealistic and you will not settle for anything less than perfect. You may put people on pedestals because you are not seeing their character clearly. Try to look at people truthfully.

Work

You may wish to become involved in humanitarian work or get involved in activities that can help you foster your spiritual ideals. Clearing out your environment of negative vibrations will help you focus and become more successful. Use your intuition in any job move. Your hunches will be correct.

Year Number	Ruling Planet	Results Throughout the Coming Year

Improving Your Luck

Be very clear in what you are trying to communicate and stick to one path this year for best results. Pay attention to your health and don't let this stress affect your positive outlook. Sleep well, exercise and develop better eating habits to allow greater energy circulation.

The 1st, 8th, 15th and 20th hours of Wednesday are your luckiest, so schedule your meetings and other important social engagements at these times.

Your lucky numbers are 5, 14, 23 and 32.

Year Number	Ruling Planet	Results Throughout the Coming Year
8	Saturn	

Overview

You have passed previous tests in life and should now be strong enough to deal with anything that life throws at you. You need to be practical and pay attention to traditional structures, and other conservative requirements.

You could become a workaholic, so pace yourself and make sure your diary is not jam-packed. Finances should improve through your efforts.

Love and Pleasure

Try not to be too serious about your relationships and keep the fun alive. Don't be too demanding and balance your professional and domestic life to keep loved ones happy. Dedicate time to your family, not just work. Schedule activities outdoors to increase your wellbeing and emotional satisfaction.

Work

Money is your focus throughout 2013, but this will require hard work on your part. You may need to make some hard decisions that could cost you friends as you choose security over outdated relationships.

Year Number	Ruling Planet	Results Throughout the Coming Year

Improving Your Luck

Being too cautious may cause you to miss opportunities during the coming 12 months. If new opportunities are offered, balance your head and your heart when drawing conclusions. You may be reluctant to attempt something new. Be kind to yourself and don't overwork or overdo exercise.

The 1st, 8th, 15th and 20th hours of Saturdays are the best times for you in 2013.

Your lucky numbers are 1, 8, 17, 26 and 35.

Year Number	Ruling Planet	Results Throughout the Coming Year
9	Mars	

Overview

In a 9 year, you will see old chapters closing and new ones opening. This may not be an easy cycle as you transition to bigger and better things. Remain open and don't hold onto the past. Do not be impulsive or irritable. Avoid arguments. Calm communication will help find solutions.

Love and Pleasure

You have strong sexual impulses during this cycle. You will enjoy your sexual intimacy. Romance is dependent on personal wellbeing, so do loads of exercise to keep fit. Receptive understanding of your lovers will bring about a new and improved state of affairs. Listen carefully to your partner's needs and try to fulfil them.

Work

This is the year when your drive and industry will provide you with excellent results. There are bigger and better things on the horizon and you will actively make them happen. You are likely to take on a leadership role and receive respect and honour from others—as long as you are fair in your dealings with them.

Improving Your Luck

Find an outlet for your high level of energy through meditation, self-reflection and prayer. Collect your energies and focus them on one point. Release tension to maintain health.

The 1st, 8th, 15th and 20th hours of Tuesday will be lucky for you throughout 2013.

Your lucky numbers are 9, 18, 27 and 36.

Mills & Boon® Online

Discover more romance at
www.millsandboon.co.uk

🌹 **FREE** online reads

🌹 **Books** up to one
month before shops

🌹 **Browse our books**
before you buy

...and much more!

For exclusive competitions and instant updates:

 Like us on **facebook.com/romancehq**

 Follow us on **twitter.com/millsandboonuk**

 Join us on **community.millsandboon.co.uk**

Visit us Online | Sign up for our FREE eNewsletter at
www.millsandboon.co.uk

WEB/M&B/RTL4